Animal Symbolism of the Chinese Zodiac

Zhang Fang

FOREIGN LANGUAGES PRESS
BEIJING

First Edition   1999

Home Page
  http://www.flp.com.cn
E-mail Addresses:
  info@flp.com.cn
  Sales@flp.com.cn

ISBN 7-119-02064-1

© Foreign Languages Press, Beijing, 1999
Published by Foreign Languages Press
24 Baiwanzhuang Road, Beijing 100037, China

Printed by Foreign Languages Printing House
19 Chegongzhuang Xilu, Beijing 100044, China

Distributed by China International Book Trading Corporation
35 Chegongzhuang Xilu, Beijing 100044, China
P.O. Box 399, Beijing, China

Printed in the People's Republic of China

Contents

I. An Introduction to the Animals of the Chinese Zodiac

This is a book that tells about the animals of the Chinese zodiac, a topic with a long history and one of great interests to the Chinese people.

Western tradition has twelve zodiac signs, each representing a month. They are Aries (the Ram), Taurus (the Bull), Gemini (the Twins), Cancer (the Crab), Leo (the Lion), Virgo (the Virgin), Libra (the Balance), Scorpio (the Scorpion), Sagittarius (the Archer), Capricorn (the Goat), Aquarius (the Water Carrier), and Pisces (the Fishes). Like the signs of zodiac, China also has twelve astrological signs. Unlike the ones in the West, however, the Chinese signs represent not only months, but years, months, days and hours. In short, the zodiac in China refers to twelve animals, each commonly used to symbolize the year in which a person is born and predicting the person's fate. The term used for the Chinese zodiac is *shengxiao*, *sheng* meaning "birth" in Chinese and here referring to the year in which a person is born; *xiao* meaning to "be like." *Shengxiao* is also called *shuxiang*, *xiang* in Chinese referring to the countenance of a person that tells his fate, and *shuxiang* meaning what kind of fate a person is destined to.

Every person is thought to be like one of the twelve animals and belongs to the fate each of them represents. The animals are the mouse, ox, tiger, rabbit, dragon, snake, horse, sheep, monkey, rooster, dog and pig, each going with one of the twelve Earthly Branches. In China, the ten Heavenly Stems (*jia, yi, bing, ding, wu, ji, geng, xin, ren, gui*) and the twelve Earthly Branches (*zi, chou, yin, mao, chen, si, wu, wei, shen, you, xu, hai*) are also used to designate years. The first year is designated by the first stem (*jia*) and the first branch (*zi*) and is thus called the year of *jiazi*.

The second year is designated by the second stem (*yi*) and the second branch (*chou*) and is called the year of *yichou*. In the same way, we get the years of *bingyin, dingmao, wuchen, jisi, gengwu, xinwei, renshen* and *guiyou* in sequence. The eleventh year is the year of *jiaxu*, which is a combination of the first stem and the eleventh branch. In this way, we can easily get the years of *yihai, bingzi, dingchou*.... Altogether there are sixty different combinations of the stems and branches to represent sixty years, which is called a *jiazi*. In one *jiazi*, twelve years are a cycle and each year is represented by one of the twelve animals, thus the years of the mouse, ox, tiger, rabbit, dragon, snake, horse, sheep, monkey, rooster, dog and pig. In conclusion, the Chinese zodiac basically refers to the twelve animals representing years and suggesting fates of people as well.

Why did people use animals to designate the years and why were these twelve animals selected? There have been different reasons cited in different dynasties. No final conclusion on the matter has yet been reached.

Originally, before animals were used to designate the years, they were used to designate different hours in a day. According to historians, it was the ethnic groups in northern China who first used animals for the years, and the practice spread from there to central China during the Eastern Han Dynasty (25-220). Before that, animals had already been used by the Han people to designate the hours. They divided one day into twelve two-hour periods, each given the name of one of the twelve Earthly Branches and labelled by one of the twelve animals. That was the original form of the Chinese zodiac, whose traces can be found in writings from ancient history. The earliest and most complete evidence for the twelve animals is found today on bamboo slips excavated in 1975 from Tomb 11 in Shuihudi, Yunmeng County, Hubei Province. Among the slips, one from the Qin Dynasty (221-206 B.C.) has figures of the twelve animals written on it. It tells of thieves stealing during different periods of a day and of the animals representing the periods. The period from 11:00

pm-1:00 am, for example, is called *zi*. So a thief in this period is described as being like a mouse with a pointed head, several whiskers, dark hands and a dark face. The twelve animals described on the bamboo slips were not all the same as the ones we have today. The period of *wu* (11:00 am-1:00 pm), for instance, was represented by a deer instead of today's horse. During the Han Dynasty (206 B.C.-A.D. 220), the animals recorded in Wang Chong's *Lun Heng* (*Discourses Weighed in the Balance*) were exactly the same as those used today. Thus we can conclude that the animals of the Chinese zodiac had emerged in embryonic form by the Qin and Han dynasties at the latest, and were originally related closely to the hours of the day. It was many years later when they were used to designate years.

Why then were these twelve animals selected? There are many different explanations for this. One of them emphasizes the habits of the animals. According to this explanation, a particular animal was selected to represent a two-hour period because it was normally active during that period.

The selection was as follows: During the *zi* period, from 11:00 pm to 1:00 am, the mouse is active; during the *chou* period, from 1:00 am to 3:00 am, the ox is ruminating; during the *yin* period, from 3:00 am to 5:00 am, the tiger is animated; during the *mou* period, from 5:00 am to 7:00 am before sunrise, the legendary jade rabbit in the moon is busy preparing medicines; during the *chen* period, from 7:00 am to 9:00 am, the dragon begins to produce rain; during the *si* period, from 9:00 am to 11:00 am, the snake becomes active; during the *wu* period, from 11:00 am to 1:00 pm, which is a period of masculinity, the horse has been selected because it is alleged to be the most masculine animal; during the *wei* period, from 1:00 pm-3:00 pm, it is said grass eaten by sheep grows fast and so the sheep has been selected; during the *shen* period, from 3:00 pm to 5:00 pm, the monkey becomes active; during the *you* period, from 5:00 pm to 7:00 pm, it becomes dark and the rooster returns home; during the *xu* period, from 7:00 pm to 9:00 pm, the watch dog is on duty; and finally, during the *hai* period, from 9:00 pm to 11:00 pm, the pig has fallen into a sound, snoring sleep.

Another explanation is based on the concept of *yin* and *yang* in ancient Chinese philosophy (*yin* and *yang* are the opposing principles in nature, the former feminine and negative, the latter masculine and positive). *Zi* is the extreme of *yin*, and is a sign of darkness and obscurity. The mouse fits here because it tends to hide itself. *Chou* is *yin*, which reminds people of a cow caressing its calves with its tongue, and so the animal that goes with *chou* is a cow, not an ox. *Yin* (the third branch) is *yang*. Too much *yang* suggests ferocity, so the tiger, which is generally looks ferocious, is put here. *Mao* and *you* represent the gateway of the sun and moon respectively. The sun is *yang* and the moon is *yin*. The rabbit takes the position the rooster should take along with *mao*, which represents the sunrise and the rooster takes the place the rabbit should take with *you*, which represents the rise of the moon. The purpose of this exchange of position is to mix *yin* and *yang*. *Chen* suggests the rise of the spirit of *yang*, so the dragon with its strong *yang* force is chosen. *Si* is similar to *chen* but is not as strong, so the snake is chosen. *Wu* is the extreme of *yang*, so the strong racing horse, representing the extreme of *yang*, is put here. *Wei* is *yin*, so the sheep is chosen here. Since a sheep kneels down to suck its mother's breast, it is also a sign of propriety. *Shen* is *yin*. Too much *yin* suggests cunningness. The monkey is chosen here because it is born to be cunning. Both *xu* and *hai* are *yin*, suggesting restraint and silence, so the peace-guarding dog and quiet pig are chosen for these position.

Though the two explanations above are both reasonable, they are somewhat far fetched. For example, there are other animals that are active during the *si* period, so why was the snake is chosen? Why was the pig is chosen to fit *hai* when many other animals are also quiet? Some researchers have tried to explore the source of the zodiac animals from tribal totems, because both the animal figures and the totems are cultural signs of a national group. Their studies have not yet succeeded because the relationship between the two is difficult to confirm.

Next comes the problem of the order of the twelve animals. The answer lies in my explanation for the relations between the hours and the animals. Here I'd like to tell an interesting story that has spread among the Chinese, although appears unscientific. We take it as part of the culture because the animals of the zodiac from the beginning were something invented and spread among the people.

The story begins with an audience held one day by the Jade Emperor (the Supreme Deity of Taoism) when the tiger, phoenix and dragon came to him to complain about how they were being bullied.

The Jade Emperor asked, "Who dares to bully you, the kings of the mountain, forest and water?"

The three answered, "It is men who always try to do us harm."

"Then," said the Jade Emperor, "go and tell your subjects to wait at the Gate of the Southern Heaven at five o'clock tomorrow morning. When I say 'Come in,' the first ten animals that come before me will be designated as man's zodiac signs and thus will never be hurt by them. I'll have no way to protect the others."

So the three hurried back to inform their subjects.

All of the animals prepared for the trip, except for the mouse, which was busy burrowing underground. When the mouse came out and saw the cat washing his face, he asked, "Why do you spend so much time washing your face? Are you going to visit your relatives or friends?"

"No," answered the cat, "I have an important thing to do early tomorrow morning."

"What is that?" asked the mouse.

The cat told the mouse everything.

"I'll go, too." said the mouse.

"Ok. Let's go together," the cat said, "Please wake me up tomorrow morning."

The mouse readily promised.

The next morning the mouse woke up at three o'clock. He thought to himself, "The cat runs faster than me. If I wake him up, he'll get there ahead of me." So he didn't wake the cat and left alone.

When he got the Gate of the Southern Heaven, he saw most of the birds and beasts waiting there. The Jade Emperor sat in his throne in the hall, asking the Great White, an official of his, to get paper and a writing brush ready. When it was five o'clock, the Jade Emperor said, "Come in!" All the animals jostled one another and no one could push to the front. The mouse realizing it was impossible to force his way through, cleverly scampered between the other animals' legs and was the first to appear before the Jade Emperor, who therefore said, "The mouse comes." The Great White then wrote down "mouse," and the mouse became the first animal of the Chinese zodiac.

The ox became impatient. He pushed past the other animals away and got to the front. The Jade Emperor said, "Here comes an ox." So the Great White wrote the name of ox in the second place.

The tiger, as strong as the ox, jumped over the other animals' heads to get in third place.

The rabbit huddled himself up and made his way through the others' legs, much like the mouse did, and got fourth place.

The dragon was very angry with the other four because he thought himself the most powerful animal. He then flew over other animals' heads by riding the clouds to get fifth place.

The snake wound its way through the other animals' legs and got sixth place.

The horse jumped forcefully up and around to get seventh place.

The sheep, not as strong as the horse, had to use its horns to gore the others and achieve eighth place.

The monkey, never one to be left behind, jumped to the front by stepping on others' heads and holding on to others' hair and ears to balance himself. He thus became the ninth.

Seeing that there were already nine in front, the rooster decided to grasp the last opportunity. He flapped his wings and flew to the front, becoming the tenth.

At this point the Jade Emperor said, "*goule* (It's enough)." The Great White mistook the word for "*gou*" (dog), and wrote down the name of the dog as eleventh. The Jade Emperor then said, "*zule* (It's enough)." The Great White mistook this for "*zhu*" (pig), and wrote down the name of the pig as the twelfth. The Jade Emperor then snatched away the list angrily and said, "Don't write any more." Since twelve animals were on the list, the Jade Emperor agreed to have twelve animals for the zodiac.

The mouse went home happily and found the cat was still washing its face. When the cat saw the mouse, it said, "It's time to go."

But the mouse answered, "Not necessary, I've already got the first place."

"Why didn't you wake me up?" asked the cat.

"How could I take first place if I had waited to wake you up?"

The cat became so angry that he sprang on the mouse. The mouse hurriedly turned and escaped. Since that time, the cat and mouse have been sworn enemies.

There are many stories such as this told among the Chinese. They have been invented to accord with the different characteristics of the animals and are an embodiment of people's likes, understanding and imagination in regard to the twelve animals. Since people like the animals of the Chinese zodiac so much, they have exerted great influence on all aspects of people's lives.

The Zodiac and Chinese Religions Confucianism, Taoism and Buddhism are the three major religions that developed in ancient China. Since the ideas of Confucianism have entered the mainstream of Chinese culture and no longer have many religious implications, Confucianism is no longer regarded as a religion. So Chinese religions here mainly refers to Taoism and Buddhism, both having countless ties with the animals of the Chinese zodiac.

The ties between the zodiac and Taoism are epitomized in the bronze sheep at Qingyang Temple, a Taoist temple in Chengdu, Sichuan Province. It is said Lao Zi, the founder of Taoism, used to ride on a black sheep to disseminate his doctrines. Though the bronze statue is called a "sheep," its body parts are composed of the twelve animals. It has a mouse's ears, an ox's nose, a tiger's paws, a rabbit's back, a dragon's horn, a snake's tail, a horse's mouth, a sheep's mustache, a monkey's jaw, a rooster's eyes, a dog's abdomen and a pig's hip. People look on it as a sacred sheep, saying that if you have an illness in any part of your body, just touch the same part on this bronze sheep and you will feel better. Besides the bronze sheep, some Taoist theories also involve the twelve animals. For example, Ge Hong, a Taoist of the Eastern Jin Dynasty (317-420), explained in his *Baopuzi* (*The Book of Master Baopu*) various Taoist rites and rules by using the Twelve Earthly Branches and the twelve zodiac animals.

Buddhism came to China from India. As its teachings spread in China, the animals of the zodiac became a part of it. According to ancient Buddhist books, Buddhism originally had twelve animals under the control of Bodhisattva. When Buddhism spread into China, the twelve animals gradually became the twelve animals of the zodiac. Originally they were all mounts for the twelve spirits: the rat for Catura, the ox for Victrola, the lion for Kumbhira, the hare for Vajra, the serpent for Andira, the horse for Anila, the sheep for Sandila, the monkey for Indra, the rooster for Pajra, the dog for Mahoraga, and the boar for Kinnara. Since these animals were similar to the twelve zodiac animals, it was easy to combine the two groups. Here is a Buddhist story about the source of the twelve animals of the Chinese zodiac:

Tathagata, the Buddhist patriarch, called all the animals to come to him before he died, but only twelve of them came. He planned to use their names to designate years according to the time of their arrival. The first who came was the cat, then the mouse, ox, tiger, rabbit, dragon, snake, horse, sheep, monkey, rooster and dog. When they arrived, Tathagata had not come yet.

The cat became impatient and slipped away. Then Tathagata arrived, but the cat was still absent. However, the pig happened to come. So the mouse became the first and the pig the last, thus forming the twelve animals of the zodiac and their order.

From stories such as this we can see that religions have had a conspicuous impact on the development of the Chinese zodiac and have enhanced the charm of it.

The Zodiac and People's Daily Life In a later chapter I'll explain the relations between the zodiac and people's daily lives in detail. Here I'm just going to give a brief compendium.

In China each person is assigned one of the twelve zodiac animals at birth, and after that every twelve years he will experience a "fate year." A person should be most careful in that year and be prepared for any contingency. In northern China, children of twelve years old are supposed to wear red underclothes in their fate years and adults are to use red girdles. This is believed to be a precaution against mishaps. In some places a person is not supposed to go out of their home on the eve of their "fate year." In other places, an old person on his birthday during his "fate year," should wear the red trousers and use the red belt presented to him by his juniors. All these precautions show how much attention people pay to their fate. Like ordinary people, high officials, even emperors, were expected to behave differently in their "fate years." Zhao Ji, an emperor of the Song Dynasty, was born in the year of the dog. In such a year he followed the suggestion of a sycophantic official and forbade his subjects to raise or kill dogs. The Empress Dowager Cixi of the late Qing Dynasty was born in the year of sheep. It is said she flew into a fury when she heard these words in an opera: "The sheep falling in a tiger's mouth will never return." In traditional China, everybody valued his fate and therefore liked one of the twelve animals related to his fate.

People sometimes are given their names according to the animals of the zodiac. Tang Yin, a great painter in the Ming Dynasty, for example, got his name because he was born in the year of the Tiger and the Tiger is correlated with the *yin* branch. He also had the style name of Bohu ("hu" means tiger in Chinese). It is popular in China to give a nickname to a child that relates to the animal the child belongs to. For instance, Xiaolong (Little Dragon), Huzai (Little Tiger), Xiaogou (Little Dog) and Xiaoniu (Little Calf), etc. People's names also correlate with the animals' habits and characteristics. For example, the mouse, ox, rabbit, horse, sheep, monkey, dog and pig eat rice and beans, so it is supposed to be good for people born in the year of these animals to have the Chinese characters for rice or bean in their names. Similarly, the ox, rabbit, horse and sheep eat grass, so it is good for people born in the year of these animals to have the Chinese character for grass in their names. The tiger eats meat, so people who are born in the year of the tiger should have the characters for meat, horse, ox, or sheep in their names. Since the tiger is the natural enemy of the ox and sheep, people belonging to the ox or sheep should not have the characters for tiger in their names. Names often suggest people's ambitions. Since the tiger is the king in the forest, a tiger person should have the character for wood, (suggesting forest) in his name. The dragon is the god of rain in Chinese mythology, so it will be good for a dragon person to have the character for water in his name.

In ancient China people thought the meat of different animals should be eaten in different seasons. According to *wuxing* identifications (the five elements of metal, wood, water, fire and earth), a year is divided into five seasons. Spring, for example, is related to wood and wood conquers earth, so animals related to earth, i.e. the ox, sheep and dog, should be eaten in spring. Chinese people have a dish named the "twelve figures," meaning that the twelve animals, from the mouse through the pig, are cooked together. Actually this cuisine is only a mixture of pork, mutton and beef, and certainly dragon meat would never in such a dish. Since people like the twelve animals very much, they often use their shapes in cooking, especially in cake-making.

In former matchmaking, a man and a woman were expected

to exchange their *bazi* (eight characters in four pairs, indicating the year, month, day and hour of a person's birth, each pair consisting of one Heavenly Stem and one Earthly Branch) to see if their fates were against each other. The zodiac animals are a part of the Eight Characters and, in Chinese folklore, certain pairs of animals came to be considered incompatible with each other. According to one scheme, the horse and the ox were bad for each other, as were the monkey and the pig, the rabbit and the dragon, the snake and the tiger, the rooster and the dog, and the sheep and the rat. Though it sounds absurd, these ideas are well rooted in traditional Chinese society. A lot of people believe in them even today.

We've talked enough about the relationships between the zodiac animals and the daily life of Chinese people, from which we've observed their core: fate. People like and worship the zodiac animals in the hope of having favorable fates. The correlated customs and habits came to be a part of ordinary Chinese good wishes. Although some things absurd and superstitious lie in these customs, and some may even called corrupt customs, they are an embodiment of China's unique national social ideology and aesthetic interest, and therefore are still attractive today.

The Zodiac Animals in Literature and Art   Since the zodiac animals are deeply rooted in traditional Chinese culture, and have been popular throughout the ages among people in all walks of life, it's natural for them to appear in literature and artistic works. Actually the amount of traditional literature and artistic creations concerning the twelve animals is spectacular. In some of them the animals and their relation to the zodiac are directly described, for example, the twelve zodiac-animal poems and pictures; in others the zodiac just plays as an episode or background of the major story. In both circumstances, writers and artists showed great interest in the zodiac animals and they nourished traditional Chinese literature and art.

First I'll discuss the twelve zodiac-animal poems. These poems were composed especially for the twelve animals. According to the historical record, a man called Li Biao of the Northern Wei Dynasty in the fifth Century composed such a poem consisting of descriptions of the twelve animals. The earliest poem about the zodiac animals found today was produced by Shen Jiong of the later Southern Dynasties. It has twelve lines, each for one of the twelve animals. The first word of each line is the name of the animal. After Shen Jiong, more people began to write poems about the zodiac animals and such poems gradually took on a style of their own. More often than not, the poems did not include all of the twelve animals, but just one or a few of them. In even more cases, animal zodiac stories appeared in the poems in the form of literary quotations.

The zodiac animals can also be found in prose. The writers usually did not mean to discuss these animals, but had other purposes. Parables and jokes can be classified in this category. Han Yu, a well-known writer of the Tang Dynasty (618-907), once wrote an article called "The Story About the Writing Brush." Because in ancient China writing brushes were often made of cony hair, the writing was actually about a rabbit. In his writing Han Yu referred to the rabbit as one of the twelve spirits, hinting at the twelve zodiac animals. Liu Zongyuan, another writer of Tang Dynasty, wrote a similar article about a mouse. The zodiac animals often appear in jokes. One of these is about two men having their meal together. One man gobbled down all his food. The other asked him what animal sign he belonged to. "Dog," the man answered. The other one said with relief, "I'm lucky today. If you belonged to the tiger, I'm afraid you would swallow me." Another joke is about a man whose birthday was soon going to come. Knowing he was born in the year of the mouse, his subordinates gave him a gold mouse as a birthday gift. The man was overjoyed with it and said, "Do you know my wife's birthday will come soon? She was born in the year of the ox."

The zodiac animals often appear in traditional Chinese plays. *Fifteen Strings of Cash* is a popular *kunqu* opera, in which the murderer and thief is called Lou Ashu (mouse). To solve the case the prefect in charge disguises himself as a glyphomancer to analyze Lou Ashu's name, telling him that the mouse is the first animal of the zodiac and therefore had to be the source of disaster. Lou Ashu panics at these words and finally is convicted.

In ancient Chinese novels, the zodiac animals are also often found. The most popular one is Pigsy, a figure with a pig's head and a human's body in *Journey to the West* by Wu Cheng'en. Before becoming a pig, Pigsy had been a marshal of troops guarding the river to heaven. Since the *hai* branch of the twelve Earthly Branches belongs to water, Pigsy must have been invented from the pig among the twelve zodiac animals.

Besides poetry, prose, plays and novels, literary descriptions of the zodiac animals are most often found in folklore and folktales. In later chapters I'll discuss this topic in detail.

Traditional Chinese sculpture also bears various zodiac animal images. Such images as tomb figures were common in ancient times. Besides, the images of these twelve animals can often be found on tomb bricks and fresco.

Folk handicrafts, such as paper-cuts, dough figures and painted eggshells, which bear the images of the twelve animals, are welcomed by ordinary people because they are inexpensive yet elegant.

Like the Han people, many of the Chinese national minorities have their own zodiac animal culture. The differences are in the animals and in their order. For the Mongolians, the twelve animals start with the tiger and end with the ox; for the Dai people, the elephant replaces the pig as the last animal; for the Li people, the rooster takes first place and the monkey is last. The Yi people substitute the dragon with a pangolin, and the Uygurs in Xinjiang substitute a fish for the dragon. In addition to the dragon substitution, the Kirgiz substitute a fox for the monkey. The folklore and traditions about the zodiac animals of the national minorities are also somewhat different from those of the Han people.

China is not the only country which has zodiac animals.

Japan's zodiac animals come from China. Like Chinese people, the Japanese love and believe in the power of these animals. Vietnam's zodiac animals are much the same as China's. The only difference is that the rabbit is replaced by the cat. Cambodia has the ox as the first and the mouse as the last animal. In Thailand, the snake is the first and the dragon is the last animal. Myanmar has eight zodiac animals, including the tiger, lion, double-tusk elephant, non-tusk elephant, mouse, cavy, dragon and bird. India's twelve zodiac animals are the mouse, ox, lion, rabbit, dragon, snake, horse, sheep, monkey, peesweep (or rooster), dog and pig.

Western countries also have symbols like China's zodiac animals. The twelve animals in ancient Greece were the rake, goat, lion, donkey, crab, snake, dog, mouse, crocodile, monkey and hawk. So zodiac animals are actually a worldwide phenomenon, and China's zodiac animals are an important part of this.

II. Tales About the Animals of the Chinese Zodiac

There are many legends, literary allusions and descriptions of the animals of the Chinese zodiac. These animals, though based on real models, do not reflect reality. Instead, their history is found in folk tales from which their cultural meanings have evolved.

1. Mouse

In China a mouse is colloquially called a *lao shu* (old mouse). Some say that this is because of the several long whiskers a mouse has that make it look old.

We have already mentioned how the mouse became the first animal of the zodiac. Another interesting story relates that Heaven and Earth were formed in the *zi* period, the first of the twelve Earthly Branches, and they were then an integrated mass. It was the mouse who took a bite out of this mass and thus separated Heaven and Earth. So the mouse is related to the *zi* period and that is why he is placed first among the twelve zodiac animals.

In the real life the mouse can be a nuisance. A Chinese folk saying describes people's disgust for mice and rats as follows: "A rat crossing the street is chased by all." But the mouse found in folk tales is quite different from those in real life. Besides its harmfulness, it has magical qualities. We should first take a look at the strange varieties of mice found in the Chinese classics to get some idea of how they are depicted in folk tales.

In *Explanation of Compositions*, there is a description of one kind of mouse that boasts five skills. It can fly but not as high as a rooftop, climb but not as high as a tree top, swim but not the width of a river, run but not as fast as people, and dig a hole but not as big as himself. These so called five skills are far from perfection. The book *Records of Miracles* mentions a kind of animal, which looks like a mouse, weighs some 5,000 kilograms, and lives under thick ice. If a person eats pemmican made from its meat, he will feel a hot sensation. A mat mall of the three-meter-long hairs of this creature can keep a person warm. When drums made from its skin are beaten, the sound can be heard even by mice one thousand *li* away and will attract them to draw near.

In the same book another kind of strange mouse is mentioned, one that weighs 500 kilograms, lives in "fire caves" and often goes out of them. It dies immediately if it is watered. Its long hairs, about one meter in length, are as fine as silk. Cloth made from them can be "washed" clean by fire. Animal which look like a mouse are also described in some books. For example, a kind of mouse, has a mouth that sticks out and is afraid of dogs. And a certain mole that is dark blue all over and has short legs and toes. It weighs more than 500 kilograms. When it shakes out its hairs in the field, the hairs turn into tiny rats that eat up all the crops. Its skin is more valuable than most leather because there are three hairs coming out of each pore. Another white mouse is white all over except for its red ears, feet and eye sockets. It is said that this red color is a reflection of the treasure it holds. The treasure can be found when its hole is burrowed into.

The above-mentioned mice with strange shapes and with strange skills are often spoken of in the ancient stories of ghosts and rarities. It seems that people have viewed the mouse as a somewhat supernatural animal, in spite of its humbleness and wretchedness. Since they both feared and admired the mouse or rat, it was natural of them to rank it among the zodiac animals. Generally speaking, such animals must have something miraculous about them in order to be included in the zodiac, and the fear of being haunted by a mouse that shows up in many tales and people's imagination is enough justification for this honor.

We may go further to see more about the unusual skills and habits of the mouse.

In the imagination of ancient people, the most important extraordinary ability of a mouse is to divine. An ancient book says that a mouse can live up to 300 years, and when it reaches 100, it will turn white all over and develop the ability to practice divination. In other words, it can foretell good and ill luck in the coming year and describe things happening thousands of *li* away. There are several ancient sayings about the magical power of mice. Among these is one that goes when mice dance at the gate of the king's palace, the state will fall; and when mice dance in the courtyard, the family of the houseowner will be drowned in disaster.

The following story gives a detailed description of the magical powers of a mouse. According to *Stories of Ghosts and Men*, a Taoist named Zhong Zuo was once lying idle at home when a mouse crept out of its hole and warned him of a coming death in next few days. Zhong Zuo told his servant to buy a dog to scare off the mouse. But the mouse said, "That won't work. If the dog comes in, it is sure to die." In a short while the words of the mouse came true. Zhong Zuo then secretly told his servant to have someone carry twenty buckets of water to his home the next day. But to his surprise, the mouse knew of his secret plan. It said to him, "Are you going to water me? Surely you'll fail in that, for my home is equipped with a convenient escape route for me." It was true and the mouse didn't get hurt at all after its hole was watered. Zhong Zuo, however, didn't abandon his plan. He had his servant call thirty people together to water the hole a second time. The mouse just smiled and said, "What's the use? If I go up and live on your roof, what can you do to me?" Zhong Zuo was at his wit's end and finally had to give up. He had a servant named A Zhou. One day the mouse told Zhong Zuo that A Zhou was going to steal 200,000 strings of coins (1,000 coins make up a string) from him and run away. Later this happened as the mouse predicted. After that Zhong Zuo began to listen in the mouse and make friends with it. He asked the mouse to bless him, and when he went out on business, he asked it to look after his house. Zhong Zuo went to sell ox leather at a place where the butchery of oxen was forbidden. He made a good fortune there. Later when he came home, he found his house intact under the protection of the mouse. Not long afterward he became an extremely rich man.

In ancient times people actually had contradictory feelings about the mouse. They imagined it to be a supernatural nymph, while at the same time they were unwilling to be controlled by it and they made up stories about men's victories over the mouse. In some of these the mouse was depicted as the defeated opponent of men and in others the mouse took on the characteristics of a man. Here is an example. According to the record in *Tales of Marvels*, there once was a lower officer named Zhou Nan who was informed of his death date by a mouse dressed in man's apparel. Zhou Nan didn't believe this disguised mouse at all. When the day came, the disguised mouse emerged again and warned Zhou, "You'll die at noon." Zhou Nan turned a deaf ear, and the mouse had to go away. At noon the disguised mouse came round again and complained, "You kept ignoring my words, and so I have no way out but die for you." With these words, the disguised mouse fell dead instantly. Zhou Nan walked near only to find that its clothes had disappeared and it looked like an ordinary mouse.

The uniqueness of the mouse lies not only in its superpowers, but also in its habits and manners. A book records the adventures of an eminent monk named Dao An. He once passed by the Kingdom of Mice on his way to the Western Regions. He found the mice there varied in size. Some were as big as dogs, some the size of rabbits, and some the size of ordinary mice. Each of them had a white head and wore a yoke around its neck. Whenever they found a passing merchant who ignored them and refused to pay homage to their god, they would gnaw at his clothes. The story gives a religious tinge to the mouse, as does another one found in another book. The story mentions a certain kind of mouse, which was a companion of a Taoist named Tang Fang. The taoist, after becoming immortal through self-cultivation, only took his rooster and dog with him to the heaven and left the forgotten mouse alone on the ground heart-broken. The mouse was so unhappy that it began to vomit its intestines in and out three times a day. Thus it got its strange name, *yichangshu* (literally means vomiting its intestines out).

Now here are some stories about the mouse's evil doings. According to *Stories of Immortals*, a man named Liu Rou once told Fu Yuzhi, a person knew Eight Trigrams, that a mouse had gnawed at his middle finger at night while he was asleep. Liu Rou asked Fu Yuzhi to explain the reason for this to him. Fu Yuzhi told him that the mouse was trying to assassinate him, and he suggested that Liu Rou have his wrist inscribed with a certain red character and then that he leave his hand outside of his quilt during the night. As expected, a big dead mouse was found beside Liu Rou's bed the next morning. Another story says that during the Wansui Period of Emperor Wu Zetian's reign (a period of the Tang Dynasty) there was a group of bandits waylaying people on the road to Chang'an at night. One night a Taoist, holding an ancient mirror, waited deliberately on the road. Not long after a team of fully armed ruffings came near. The Taoist suddenly mirrored them. The bandits turned tail and fled. But the Taoist didn't stop his hot pursuit for them until he reached a big hole. He had this dug up only to find more than one hundred big mice hiding there. Obviously it was the mice that were the bandits. They were killed immediately, and after that the road became safe. Here is one more story. Someone once lost his daughter and kept looking for her for more than one year, but in vain. One day he heard a baby crying under the ground. He was so surprised that he began to dig into the earth around a small hole. The hole became bigger as he dug at it. At last he revealed a sight that almost caused him to faint—his daughter sitting beside a big bald mouse, who was sure to be her husband, with their new-born baby in her arms. Obviously it was the mouse which had seduced her into marrying it. Such stories, most of which are woven around the evil nature of mice, are frequently found in ancient books. The mouse, of course, has done a lot of harmful things to men and therefore it usually plays the role of vermin in these stories.

But there are exceptional tales, about mice's good deeds as well, such as one about the hundreds of mice suddenly appeared in Cui Huaiyi's courtyard walking on two legs. This prompted the members of the Cui family to hurry out of the house and have a look. They had hardly gotten outside when their house collapsed. Thus the whole family was saved. According to *Investigation of Spirits*, an army officer named Chai Zaiyong liked to sit alone in his reception hall. One day a mouse ran up to him and bowed. Chai Zaiyong was disgusted by it and drove the mouse outside. Just at that moment a beam in the hall broke and fell down on the very spot where he had been sitting. It seems that the mouse acted to save him from danger, perhaps because of its super powers at divination.

Thus the stories about mice and rats show that they do good deeds as well as harm to man. The mice in these stories can save people's lives, and they know how to return the hospitality they have received from people. During the Ming Dynasty a story circulated about a mouse and an examination paper. According to this story, when a civil service examiner was once selecting qualified papers, one of his discarded papers was secretly retrieved and returned to the qualified list. Greatly surprised, he again discarded the paper and then pretended to be asleep so that he could watch what was going on. He soon found that some mice were retrieving the paper and placing it in the qualified pile. In order to know more, the curious examiner decided to pass the paper and later asked the examinee, "Did your forefathers follow a virtuous path all their lives so that even the mice are willing to help you?" The young man answered, "I'm really not clear about my forefathers' virtues deeds, but one thing I know is that we haven't raised cats for three generations." No wonder the well-protected mice wanted to help the young man.

Stories about mice are not only found in tales and mythology, they also are found in books of philosophy where they serve to vividly explain profound philosophical concepts. For example, a philosophy book, *The Book of Master Lie*, mentions a fable about a putrid mouse. This says that once in the state of Liang there was a rich man named Yu, who was quite ostentatious and extravagant. One day he invited some friends to make merry with him. As they were shooting arrows at birds for the fun of it, a putrid mouse fell down from a wounded bird's mouth on top of the head of a passing nobleman. The nobleman, in a violent rage, said to his companion, "The rich guy always turns up his nose at the others, and this time he has insulted me by hitting me on the head with a putrid mouse. How dare he! Don't think for a moment that I will allow him to survive beyond tomorrow!" The nobleman quickly mustered some people to attack the richman's house and managed to kill all the Yus. Perhaps the moral of this fable can be summarized by an old Chinese saying: "Human fortunes are as unpredictable as the weather." It also teaches one to behave in a modest manner, which ensures a safer life.

Some characters and events recorded in history books are also related to mice, as these often served as foils for heroes and historical events. For example, *Records of the Historian* tells the story of an oppressive official named Zhang Shang. Once during his childhood, his father told him look after the house. In the father's absence, Zhang Shang failed to keep all things intact, and a mouse came and stole meat from the kitchen. When Zhang Shang's father returned and learned of this, he gave his son a sound beating. Zhang Shang then made up his mind to find the thief. Later he managed to dig out the very mouse and the stolen meat. Excitedly, he set up a clandestine tribunal to interrogate the mouse and sentence it to death. His father looked in on the "trial" and was surprised to find that his son was as skilled as any veteran jailer. This case influenced Zhang Shang's character and his future career a great deal.

Besides such stories, there are some tales of historical figures and their relation to the mouse. For instance, in *The History of the Jin Dynasty* there is an anecdote about a person named Huang Jiuyue. It says at the eve of his birth, his mother dreamed of a mouse with a pearl in its mouth. As luck would have it that was the year of mouse. Although such a coincidence cannot be taken as credible, it does show the profound influence of the zodiac signs on people's lives and mind-set. And for this reason, the humble and ugly mouse is also a favorite theme in literature. Bu Pu, a man of letters during the Jin Dynasty, wrote odes (short-versed prose) for various strange mice. In his Ode to a Flying Mouse, he describes a super creature that soars into the sky by using its whiskers, is kept flying by its tail, and travels mysteriously without leaving any trace behind.

As we have said before, the historical and cultural tales endowed some animals with supernatural power, so in time these animals became listed among the Zodiac group. The mouse or rat, generally an evil-doer with ugly looks, was the luckiest of all because it took first place.

2. Ox

The ox is much loved by the Chinese people both in actual life and in traditional culture because it is closely related to the survival and perpetuation of human beings. Truly, human civilization would not have evolved to its present stage without oxen. China is an agricultural country with land cultivation taking the lead from ancient times to the present. In this, the ox has always played an important role. In addition, the ox is much loved by people because of its characteristics—plain, diligent and conscientious, hard working, and rarely harmful to people. People therefore love to sing the praises of the ox through their tales, stories, ballads, and other artistic forms. In fact the ox is one of the animals most widely depicted in China's traditional culture.

The ox is probably the animal most directly related to Chinese history among the twelve signs of the zodiac. In terms of Chinese writing along the ox has made a great contribution as a major carrier of history and culture. Ox bones, along with tortoise shells, were used during the Shang Dynasty—the earliest with a written language—to record the results of an ancient form of fortune telling. The ox bones were burned over a fire and then the cracks thus produced were studied to determine the results of such shells with ancient characters, or words, on them have been found at many archaeological sites in China. They record the history of the ancient people's life and work, as well as their primitive concepts of nature and society. Therefore, one will surely remember the ox when reviewing the origin of China's civilization.

As human civilization progressed, the ox played an increasingly important role. It was used in cultivation by farmers, in transportation by businessmen, as food, and for sacrificial rites that had a deep influence on Chinese culture. Sacrificial rites were among the most important and sacred activities in people's lives during ancient times, and people regarded them as a means for linking themselves to nature—or more precisely, as a way of praying to the gods so that the gods might bless them. Articles used in such sacrificial rites needed to be the best ones in people's lives, and people regarded the ox as their most important animal. This is recorded in various books on rites and regulations. For example, a special kind of ox was used for offering sacrifices to heaven, earth or to an ancestor. People with different positions in society would use different kinds of oxen when offering sacrifices.

However, the killing was actually quite cruel, and often aroused people's sympathy. According to the *Mencius*, King

Xuan of Qi said sadly, when he saw an ox being led for the purpose of offering a sacrifice, "I cannot bear to see the ox die pitifully. Let's use sheep instead." It was also cruel to kill sheep, of course, but people had such a close relationship with and deep affection for the ox that it seemed less of a tragedy to kill sheep. The ox also didn't want to be sacrificed, though it was treated honorably before its death. As noted in the *Zhuang Zi*, "have you ever seen an ox used to offer a sacrifice? It wears beautifully embroidered clothes, and eats excellent food. However, it is not even as lucky as a calf without people's care when it is led into the Imperial Ancestral Temple to be killed."

Because the ox had so many uses, organizations for raising oxen were controlled by the State. The men who raised oxen were called cowherds, and the raised oxen, "public oxen." These oxen, used on different occasions, had various names according to their uses. Those used for sacrifices were called "sacrificial oxen"; those used to entertain guests, "dietary oxen"; those used in funerals, "memorial oxen"; those used as provisions for troops during war, "reward oxen"; and those used in marches and battles, "chariot oxen." We can see from the above that the ox played an important role in the social activities during China's ancient times when the forces of production were not very developed. The success and failure of many important historic events were often decided by an ox, and it played a most splendid role in war.

The ox sometimes acted to prevent war. According to the *Zuo Qiuming's Commentary on the Spring and Autumn Annals*, the State of Qin once dispatched troops to suppress the State of Zheng. Xuan Gao, a businessman of the State of Zheng, met the Qin troops on his way to visit other states on business. An idea occurred to him. He gave twelve excellent oxen to the Qin troops as a gift and told them that on hearing that the Qin troops were going to pass the State of Zheng, the King of the State of Zheng had decided to specially offer them as a gift. Hearing this, the commander of the Qin troops thought that the action plan had been discovered by their rivals, so he withdrew the troops and went back to the capital. In this way, the twelve oxen successfully prevented a war. Sometimes, however, oxen were directly involved in war. According to the *Records of the Historian,* a general named Tian Shan ordered his men to tie sharp swords on the horns of over a thousand oxen, and burn fires at the tails so they would run forward. The general dressed the oxen in colorful clothes. They assaulted at the front in the battle, with their incomparably sharp swords and the flames at their tails springing up to heaven. The troops followed. Their rivals suffered a disastrous defeat.

Oxen were more frequently used as a means of transport. They were used to carry munitions and provisions during wars all the way up to modern times. Zhuge Liang, a resourceful strategist during the Three Kingdoms Period, once invented a "wooden ox," that greatly convenienced war transport. This ox, of course, no longer exists, but according to Zhuge Liang's descriptions it had a square body, crooked head, four feet on one leg. Its head shrank into its neck, and its stomach could hold many objects for battle. It was a highly efficient means of transport at that time, and may be regarded as a special member in the ox family.

Although the ox had many practical uses, people's knowledge of it was not restricted to these. They also gave oxen a marvelous and romantic flavor. The oxen of fables and legends had special characteristics, origins, appearances and functions that could only exist in people's imaginations.

According to Taoist legends, the black ox was the favorite means of transport for Taoist priests, and it is said that the spirit of the black ox came from a 10,000-year-old tree. One book tells a story of Taoist priest named Feng Junda went to Niaoshu Mountain when he was young to cultivate himself according to the Taoist doctrines, and he returned to his hometown one hundred years later. As he often rode a black ox, he was called the Taoist Priest Riding a Black Ox. The relationship between the black ox and Taoism originated with Lao Zi, the founder of

Taoism. Legend has it that Lao Zi once had to go through a strategic pass, and the defending officer told the guard, "If you see an old man riding a cart pulled by a black ox, please do not let him pass, and inform me immediately." On that day, an old man riding a cart pulled by a black ox did appear, and the guard told the officer about it immediately. The officer then said happily, "I am going to meet the sage." He went out right away to take the old man as his teacher. The old man was none other than Lao Zi. Later Taoist believers became fond of riding black oxen in their attempt to imitate Lao Zi.

There are also legends about a golden ox and a silver ox that could produce gold or silver. It was said that during the reign of Emperor Wu Di of Western Han, a farmer in Jinniugang, a place in the southwest of Changsha City, asked a fisherman riding in a boat to carry him and his red ox across the river. The fisherman said, "The boat is too small to carry the ox," but the farmer answered, "Don't worry about it. It's not very heavy." At this, the fisherman permitted the farmer and his ox to embark on his boat. When the boat came to the middle of the river, the ox defecated into it and the farmer said to the fisherman, "The ox excrement is for you." The fisherman, of course, was very angry as the two left the boat for he thought the ox's excrement made his boat dirty. It was only after he had shoveled most of the excrement into the river that he suddenly discovered it was gold. Then he realized that the farmer and his ox were gods. But they had already disappeared into the deep mountains. In the *Miscellany of the Youyang Mountains*, there is a story about a silver-producing ox that also took place during the reign of the Emperor Wu Di of Western Han. A man riding a white ox passed Yinniu Mountains, which lay in the north of Taiyuan County, and trod on some of farmland. The farmer who owned the land became quite angry at this, but the man said, "I am the envoy of Beihai Lake, and I am going to the mountains to see the Emperor offering sacrifices to heaven and earth." Then he went on into the mountains, riding the ox. Surprised, the farmer asked others to go into the mountains with him to search for the man and his ox. However they could no longer find him and only discovered the excrement of the ox which had now turned into silver.

To the ancient people the scenery of the western regions was often mysterious in its color and the area harbored strange and mysterious oxen. Legend has it that there was an ox in the state of Dayuezhi in the western regions. If its flesh was cut away, it would grow again the next day. It is also said that there was a calf living in the mountains in the state of Xinchang that often shared its cave with a snake. The *Miscellany of the Youyang Mountains*, also says that there was a wild ox living in the western regions that was approximately three meters long. It had white hair, and its head and tail looked like those of a deer. All these tales may have some basis in reality, but most probably the stories of these magical animals were invented by people attracted by the mysterious nature of the mountains.

In some areas, the ox was treated as a god rather than just a magical animal. During the Warring States Period, Li Bing, the magistrate of Chengdu, Sichuan, made history by building great water conservancy projects. According to a wide-spread fairy tale about him, there was a river god in the region who insisted on marrying two little girls each year. With the interests of the people at heart, Li Bing decided to marry his own daughter to the river god. On the wedding day, Li Bing went to the temple where the marriage was to take place to scold the river god for its harmful deeds. Then both Li Bing and the river god disappeared suddenly. After quite a while, people saw two oxen having a ferocious battle on the river bank. Li Bing returned in the anteroom to tell his subordinates that the ox to the south with white color on its waist was him. The subordinates stabbed the ox to the north to death. That was the river god. There is another legend about an ox as a tree god. According to the *Tales of Marvels*, Duke Wen of Qin had his men cut down a catalpa tree, and when they did so it turned into an ox. Prince Wen of Qin ordered his men to pursue it. But the ox entered the water, submerged itself, and never appeared again. The Qin people established a memorial temple, which was said to be the origin of all the later ox-king temples. Many such temples were erected to enshrine and worship the ox god. People would go to these temples to offer sacrifices to the ox king on the first day of October by the lunar calendar, repaying the ox's contributions to agricultural production. The ox king, of course, was only a symbol for the tens of thousands of oxen used in farming.

Among the fairy tales about the ox, the story of "the Cowherd and the Weaving Maid" is a most beautiful and touching one. According to this legend, a weaving maid, who was originally the seventh fairy maiden in the heavenly palace, and came to earth to have a look. She fell in love with Dong Yong, a poor yet sincere and honest young man. They fell in love, got married, gave birth to two children, and lived a happy life. However, the seventh fairy maiden had violated the laws of the god in heaven by descending to earth. The god of the heaven ordered that she be brought back to heaven. Dong Yong desperately pursued her, carrying their son and daughter with him. When he was about to catch up, the god of the heaven drew a line between the two of them and a large river then appeared there, separating the couple forever. The god of the heaven only allowed the couple to meet once every year on July 7 when many magpies would join together to form a bridge so that they could cross over and meet each other. This is termed "to meet on the magpie bridge." At other times the weaving maid had to weave on one side of the river while the cowherd took care of cattle on the other side. If one looks up at the sky at night, one can see the stars named Altar and Vega facing each other across the "river," which is the Milky Way. Ancient storytellers also invented other fairy tales about the two lovers. It is said that there was a man who lived on the coast who could see a large ship sailing towards the seashore every year in August by the lunar calendar. One August he prepared some food and boarded the ship. Several days passed before it reached a place that had many houses in which several women were weaving. He also saw there a man leading an ox to drink water. When the man returned home, he told Yan Junping, an astrologer, about this event. Yan Junping said that, according to his analysis there were stars of unknown origin drawing close to Altar at that time. This trip of the man's to the Milky Way was proof to ancient people that the legend about the Cowherd and the Weaving Maid was indeed a true story.

There are other stories concerning an ox, however, that are full of the sense of strength show a striking contrast to the love story of the Cowherd and the Weaving Maid. One of these is about how the king of Qin opened a road to the State of Shu during the Warring States Period. The king of Qin wanted to defeat and eliminate the State of Shu, but he could find no way to go there because of the high mountains and lofty hills separating the Shu territory from the Central Plains. So the king of Qing ordered his men to carve five huge stone oxen, behind which he put several pieces of gold. He then spread the rumor that they were celestial animals that could produce gold. The king of Shu took this to be true and sent five men of unusual strength to pull the five oxen to his palace. Three of them were brought in this way to Chengdu, capital of the Shu State. Thus a road was opened up through which the Qin troops could travel to attack the State of Shu.

Stories such as "the Cowherd and the Weaving Maid" and "Five Men of Unusual Strength Pulling Oxen" did not describe the actions of oxen themselves, but the importance of the ox as a symbol. It had great meaning because of its close relationship to people's lives, emotions and ideals. The lives of many famous people in China's history are also related to the ox. Bai Lixi, a famous prime minister during the Spring and Autumn Period and the Warring States Period, lived by selling oxen before he rose to a position of power, while Ning Qi, another well-known prime minister, was put in charge of feeding oxen at a time when he was in dire straits. Their honors and disgrace, successes and failures were tightly bound to the ox. The lives of some artists were also vitally interrelated with oxen. For example, Wang Mian, a painter during the Yuan Dynasty, herded cattle in his childhood and learned to paint in the intervals. Besides people, many of China's place names have the character for "ox," and therefore were somewhat related at one time to oxen. The Huangniu (yellow ox) Gorge on the Yangtze River is said to have received help from a yellow ox when Yu the Great, founder of the Xia Dynasty, was regulating rivers and watercourses. The Huangniu Shoal in that gorge is flanked on its south bank by high mountains at the top of which is a stone wall. According to ancient books, the stone wall was carved with a picture of a man shouldering a sword and leading a yellow ox. However, there was no road leading to the mountain, and the origin of the murals remains to this day a mystery. There are many places named by ox, and each has its own story about an ox.

3. Tiger

Known as the king of animals, the tiger is a large beast of prey. It is born with markings on its forehead that resemble the character for "king," and as an animal it looks somewhat like a real king. In traditional Chinese culture, the image of tiger was always connected with dignity and power. For example, the design of tiger can be often found in the bronze ware of the Shang Dynasty, on a type of wine vessel known as a *zun*. The *zun* was not only a wine vessel, but it was also a symbol for dignity. Certainly, the image of a tiger has a deterrent force. There was also the *fu*, a tiger-shaped tally issued to generals as the imperial authorization for troops. Half of the *fu* was kept in the hands of the king, half in the hands of the general. Only when the two halves met, could the troops be mobilized. In folk tales, the tiger was not always related to power, but it could indicate powerful strength. It was said that the door-god fed ghosts to tigers after catching them, so some people made the tiger into a door-god. Even a cloth toy tiger was used to prevent ghosts. It would be put beside a child's pillow to prevent the child from being frightened. Many families, especially families of high standing and influence, liked to have a large painting of a tiger in their main hall so as to show the breadth of their spirit.

. In fairy tales, the tiger was more closely related to the lives of human beings than to a symbol of dignity and power. In other words, the tiger that symbolized power and dignity was a rigid object, but the one in fairy stories is vivid, fresh and full of human characteristics because it embodied people's feelings and imagination.

In the *Record of the Country South of Mount Huayang* by Chang Qu of the Eastern Jin Dynasty (317-420), King Zhao of the Qin recruited brave men, by offering them high pay, to kill an evil white tiger. Several of the men shot the tiger leaving three arrows in its head. Usually there was a group of other tigers that followed the white tiger wherever it went, but because it was ashamed of its defeat by the brave archers, the white tiger killed all its followers and died with a roar. This story expresses the heroic and stirring spirit of a tiger rather than harm to human beings because it is a story in which men overcame the tiger. More often the stories tell of people being killed by tigers. A tale says that an official named Liu Guangya passed by a place where many tigers lived. With much care, he tethered an ox and a horse in front of him, put a halberd beside him and slept among a group of people at night. But he was still picked out by a tiger. It seems it was hard for the people who lived in ancient society to guard against tigers because tigers are much stronger than people.

Strangely, though humans are enemies of the tiger in many fairy tales, both could sometimes change their roles; that is to say, people could became tigers and tigers could become people. The book *Stories of Immortals* written by Gan Bao of the Eastern Jin Dynasty, tells a story that a person used cage to catch tigers. One day he saw a low-ranking official wearing an official hat was inside the cage. He asked what happened. The official said, "Yesterday I entered this cage on the way to do business and have been unable to get out since." The hunter immediately opened the cage to let the man out. Unexpectedly, the official became a tiger and ran away as soon as he got out of the cage. So the tiger could turn into a human in order to cheat people. Another story tells how people could become tigers. When a boy pastured a cow, the cow began to lick him. The licked part of the boy's body become white and the child died not long afterward. His family later killed the cow to provide a feast for their guests. Over twenty people who ate parts of the cow turned into tigers.

A more fantastic story tells about a tiger marrying a woman. It is said that a tiger changed into a man and then married a woman. They lived in the remote mountains after the marriage. Two years passed, and the woman still had no idea that her husband was a tiger. Then one day, two guests visited them with a gift of wine. The tiger said to his wife, "You'd better not steel a glance, for the guests are eccentric." The wife was puzzled by this statement, and so she came to have a look after her husband and the guests had become drunk. She was amazed to see that they were all tigers. When the tiger woke up, he asked his wife "Did you steel a glance?" The wife lied in saying that she did not. Some days later, she asked her husband to go with her to visit her parents. The couple took a gift of wine and meat for them. They had to cross a river near the wife's home. The wife crossed first. When her husband took of his clothing to cross the river, the wife asked him, "Why did a tiger's tail appear on your backside?" The tiger felt ashamed at this and ran into the remote mountains never to return. It is interesting that in this story that the ferocious tiger departs from its violent nature, lives like humans, and doesn't want revenge after its true colors are revealed. The story has something in common with the tales of the Greek gods of Olympus who liked to lure women into marriage. It shows that in fairy tales the terrible king of animals can be given a human nature.

Perhaps because of this people relate to tigers more readily than they do to other dangerous animals. People have no problem, for example, with using the word tiger for place names. Take beautiful Suzhou and Hangzhou. There is a Chinese saying that goes "Paradise is above and Suzhou and Hangzhou below," which suggests that the landscape of these two places is the best found under heaven. One famous site at Suzhou is called Tiger Hill. This is where the King of the Wu State, Fu Chai, buried his father, He Lü. It is said that a white tiger appeared three days after the funeral. Hence the name of Tiger Hill. Also, there is a Tiger Running Spring at West Lake in Hangzhou. It is said that an eminent monk of the Tang Dynasty lived here and suffered from lack of water. One day two tigers came to this place to dig a hole. After that a clear and sweet spring came out of the ground. Visitors are not frightened by the fact that tiger is part of the names for both sites. In Chinese idioms, tiger and wolf or tiger and leopard often go together, such as "a tiger-like, wolfish disposition." Most of these idioms express violent and evil behavior. The concepts of wolf and leopard are frightening. Their nature is to eat people and other animals such as poultry. A close relationship has never been built between people and wolves and leopards even in fairy tales and literary works. But the tiger is different, even though it is sometimes harmful to people. People still like to imagine it to be an amiable animal. It is quite popular for Chinese children to wear tiger-head shoes. They do not feel frightened of them at all. Yet would children dare to wear shoes that embodied a wolf or a leopard? Moreover, the tiger has always played a different role from the wolf or leopard in works of art. In paintings a tiger appears again and again, but a wolf or a leopard can be seldom found. So it is in literary works. Take, for example, the famous story "Wu Song Kills a Tiger" from *Outlaws of the Marsh*. The fight depicted there is breath-taking, but the tiger is not terrible. It rather sets off Wu Song's heroic spirit. And the vivid description of tiger is much stronger than its violent nature. In the later Peking Operas, the tiger becomes a completely artistic figure. But in traditional Chinese culture and art, we can find no similar examples for the wolf or the leopard.

All this shows that tiger has been humanized in Chinese traditional culture. It is unique for this to happen with a large beast of prey. Thus it has become one of the twelve animals of the zodiac, used to symbolize the year in which a person is born. Those beasts of prey that aren't among these twelve animals, including the wolf and the leopard, have no such characteristics, although they are all violent and harmful to people. One more example. According to some folk tales, the tiger was called General Yin or General Calico Yin. Yin is the position in which the tiger stands among the twelve animals of the zodiac. A story is told of a scholar who lived in the remote mountains by himself. One night someone knocked his door calling himself General Calico Yin. After the two of them sat down, they drank wine and composed poems, and then said goodbye to each other after thoroughly enjoying themselves. The scholar found a tiger's footprint outside his door in the next morning. Thus he realized that a tiger could turn into a gentle and cultivated scholar.

4. Rabbit

The image of the rabbit is perhaps the most lovely one of the twelve symbolic animals. With soft skin and fur, long ears, timid eyes, and compliant character, the rabbit is never depicted as being opposed to other animals. So the image of a rabbit always suggests something beautiful to the imagination. The rabbit is particularly charming because of its connection with the most beautiful woman of legend.

This woman was called Chang'e. She was the wife of Houyi, a hero who was a skillful archer. Chang'e flew to the moon after secretly eating her husband's elixir which was given by the Queen Mother of West. From then on, she led a lonely life there because there were only three living things on the moon: Wu Gang, a man who was punished for chopping down a tree; the Jade Rabbit, who kept pounding preparations of medicine, and an idle frog. People show their sympathy for the fate of Chang'e, but at the same time, the Jade Rabbit has also become lovingly pathetic.

The Jade Rabbit was the earliest object to give the moon mythological meaning. The great poet of the Warring States Period, Qu Yuan, speaks of the rabbit in the moon in his poem

"Asking the Heaven." A later writer mentions in his poem that the Jade Rabbit pounded medicine on the moon. All these images are based on the theory of *yin-yang* and the five elements and twelve Earthly Branches, used in combination with the Heavenly Stem to designate years, months, days and hours. In the view of ancient people, the sun had the essence of *yang*. Birds would appear when its vital essence was strong enough. So the golden bird that belonged to *yang* lived in the sun. The moon had the essence of *yin*. Beasts would appear when its vital essence was strong enough. So the Jade Rabbit, which belonged to *yin*, lived on the moon. Some people said that the rabbit was related to the moon because it is at the position of *mao* in the twelve Earthly Branches, when the moon is the fullest. This explanation associates it with the twelve animals of Chinese zodiac, and the origin of the twelve animals is closely related with the twelve Earthly Branches. That, then, is the relationship between the rabbit and the moon.

The moon is clear and quiet, full of tenderness and poetic conception, while the sun has always been related to heroes with lofty ideals in Chinese mythology, persons such as Houyi shooting the sun and Xihe riding the sun. The moon always appears as light and bright in fairy tales. This meets the aesthetic forms of *yin* and *yang* in Chinese classic philosophy. Because the image and disposition of the rabbit belonged to the essence of *yin*, it was natural to connect it with the moon.

Let's now come back to the ground and find out what happened to the rabbit on earth. Of course the following are all the result of imaginings by people.

Although the rabbit is a common animal, but mysterious colors were often added to it. *Records in Past and Present* by Cui Bao of the Western Jin Dynasty says in the first year of the reign of Emperor Chengdi of the Han Dynasty, a white rabbit with red eyes was caught in a place called Shanyang. It was regarded as a monster, perhaps because of its red eyes and so the ancient book recorded it. A more fantastic rabbit is found in fairy tales. *The*

Classic of Mountains and Rivers says that there was a kind of rabbit on Mount Tianchi that had a mouse-like head and could fly by the hair on its back. In Taoism, the rabbit was regarded a kind of mythical being. It could live for one thousand years. When it was five hundred years old, its body became white. As a fairy being, it could help people to become immortal. Thus in Taoist alchemy, the rabbit was used in medicine. For example, a mixture of rabbit's blood, an elixir pill and honey which was steamed for one hundred days could prolong life.

The rabbit's uniqueness, in fact, was shown not only in fairy tales and Taoism, but also in folk culture. It was said that the rabbit's propagation relied not on its mating ability but on its watching the moon, that is, the female rabbit got essence from the Jade Rabbit by watching the moon and thus obtained the ability to reproduce. Another version says that the female rabbit became pregnant by licking a male rabbit's fur, and she then vomited a baby rabbit. There was, of course, no proof for such beliefs, but the rabbit's strong propagation ability made people think of such explanations and that's why the rabbit symbolized a flourishing population in popular culture.

In people's minds, the rabbit is an auspicious animal. An ancient book on the relationship of heaven to humans regarded a red rabbit as a particularly auspicious animal. Whenever a king of a state exhibited strong merit and virtues, a red rabbit would arrive. In ancient wars there were fleet horses that were called "red rabbits." One such was Lü Bu's "red rabbit" horse, as described in *The Three Kingdoms*. It could run as quickly as a rabbit and, at the same time, people hoped it would bring luck to its owner. In popular culture, the rabbit's leg bone was quite auspicious, so people who ate this part of it at a meal were considered very lucky.

In ancient philosophy and historical works, the rabbit often was a figure of fable. One famous tale is "Stand by a Stump Waiting for More Rabbits" from *Han Fei Tzu*. It tells of a farmer ploughing in a field who saw a rabbit kill itself by crashing into a tree trunk. Because the farmer thus got a free rabbit to eat, he gave up working and waited for another one to kill itself the next day. But after that no more rabbits crashed into the tree at all. This fable warned people who want to get by without doing any labor not to count on enjoying fruits of others' work, but to make efforts by themselves. Another fable warned people not to fight each other or else a third person might benefit. Han Lu was the bravest dog in the world, and Dongguo Wei, the smartest rabbit under heaven. In order to chase Dongguo Wei, the dog ran around a big mountain three times and climbed up and down five times. At last, neither animal could move at all. A farmer saw them and caught both of them without striking a blow. This fable comes from *Records of the Warring States*, a history of the Warring States Period. The sage Chunyu Kun told the tale to the King of Qi when the State Qi was preparing to attack the State of Wei.

In fairy tales, the rabbit always played a gentle and cultivated role, but sometimes it assumed a terrible shape. According to *Investigation of Spirits*, a high-ranking official named Yang Mai said he liked to hunt when he was young. Once when he was going to the outskirts of the city to hunt with his eagle, he saw a rabbit jumping in the distance. He set his eagle free to catch it. The rabbit disappeared when the eagle got close. After Yang Mai called his eagle back and went further, he saw the rabbit again. He again let his eagle go, but the same thing happened, and so it did again and again. He thought this strange and asked people to cut the grass away. He then found the bones of a rabbit. What he had actually seen was a rabbit ghost. In the sketchbook *Brief Records of Contemporary News* by Zhang Zhuo of the Tang Dynasty, a place called Lansheng was infested with rabbits. Tens of thousands of them ate up all the crops and then vanished without a trace. It is thought that rabbit were also ghosts sent to make trouble.

Although there are some worthless rabbits in legends, generally speaking the rabbit is loved by people. Some people even regard the features of a rabbit as a reflection of morality. For example, a rabbit sometimes appears, sometimes disappears, which in the case of the auspicious red rabbit, symbolizes whether a king has merits or not. A rabbit is also sometimes fast, sometimes slow, which indicates the rule of movement and motionlessness. And its white look can be a standard for humans. All these ideas put more of a cultural conception into the image of the rabbit.

5. Dragon

As the only imaginary animal among the twelve symbols of the zodiac, the image of the dragon is found in pictures, carvings and writings. In ancient times nobody had any doubts about the existence of dragons. People showed great respect for any dragon depicted in pictures, carvings and writings, and as a result the dragon became the symbol of Chinese nation. In modern times some people have begun to study the origin of dragon. Some think the concept of the dragon may have come from a snake, fish, or lizard, and perhaps some other animal. In the minds of the early Chinese people, the dragon was a god that embodied the will and ideals of the Chinese people. One book says that the dragon is a large-scaled reptile, which can become dark or bright, large or small, long or short, and can fly into the sky in the spring and live under the water in the fall. It seems that the dragon is capable of doing almost anything. All people in China, including the emperor, prostrated themselves before the image of a dragon with reverence and awe. As a result, this unreal animal became the spiritual sustenance for a nation: firstly, as the totem of a tribe and then as the symbol of the nation. Eventually it became the sign on the national flag of the last feudal dynasty, the Qing Dynasty. The Chinese people regard themselves as descendants of the dragon.

Today we don't think of it as a god or symbol, so let's have a look at what the dragon was in Chinese history and culture.

First, let's see what kind of images and powers were given to the dragon by ancient people. Ancient books mention different kinds of dragons, such as the flood dragon with scales, the dragon with wings, the dragon with horns and the dragon without horns. The different dragons had different functions. For example, living under water, the flood dragon was a water god. When residing in the water it had numerous powers and it did nothing without water. In some ancient books, the dragon which did not fly to heaven was called a curled-up dragon. It is said that it had a more than thirteen-meter-long body of black and green color with a red line along its middle that looked like silk. It often swam along the Wei River to the sea. If it hurt anybody, the person would die immediately. All the above dragons appeared in lexico graphical works and historical records. There were other strange dragons in fairy tales. In *Classic of Mountains and Rivers*, there was a candle dragon with a length of one thousand five hundred kilometers. When it opened its eyes, daytime came; when it closed its eyes, night fell.

In fairy tales, there was also a state of dragons—the so-called dragon pool. Located on a mountain, the pool had a circumference of three hundred and fifty kilometers. This is where many dragons live. Their food was a five-flower tree grown in dragon pool. In the case of immortals, the dragon was used to set off their mystery by contrast. For example, the Queen Mother of the West in one fairy tale rode a nine-colored, spotted dragon cart. No doubt, riding in a dragon cart was the symbol of her supremacy. In reality, only the emperor could ride in a dragon cart. It was said that an emperor of the Xia Dynasty, named Qi, rode in a two-dragon cart through the outskirts of the city. But this, of course, was just a legend. Yet the emperors proclaimed themselves dragons, and the sons of the heaven.

The people accepted the fact that emperors were dragons and sons of heaven, but in their minds the real dragon was not only the emperor but also sages with high prestige, such as Confucius. Although he was not an emperor, people regarded him as an emperor who never took the throne. It is said that the night Confucius was born, two black dragons arrived at his mother's room. After his birth, two goddesses washed his mother's body. In the view of ancient people, Confucius was so great that he could not have been a mortal. That's why they developed such an interpretation of Confucius. That is to say, Confucius was also a dragon and the son of the heaven.

But Confucius had a different view. He considered dragons to be people who had a different view. He considered dragons to be people who had freed themselves from worldly cares. It is said that Confucius called Lao Zi a dragon. In this way, all celebrated people might be called dragons. For instance, in the Wei State of the Three Kingdoms Period celebrated people such as Hua Xin, Bing Yuan and Guan Ning were good friends. They were called dragons by people, Hua Xin was called the dragon's head, Bing Yuan, the dragon's body, and Guan Ning, the dragon's tail. One more example. Huang Shang and Ji Yuanli were also outstanding people of that time. They both married daughters of General Huan Wen. People said that the two daughters of Huan Wen rode the dragons, which meant the two daughters had husbands like dragons. That's why people called the ideal son-in-law the riding-dragon son-in-law in later ages.

Let's return to some of the stories about dragons. We mentioned earlier Emperor Qi's riding a dragon, but his father, Yu, was even protected by dragons. Because Yu ran the country well and was strong in virtuous, two dragons from the heaven were sent down to pull the cart for him. Yu visited the south by riding the dragon cart. The god who was in charge of preventing the wind begrudged Yu's presence and wanted to shoot him. However, two dragons rose high into the air with a roar of thunder. The god who was in charge of preventing the wind was so frightened that he killed himself by thrusting a knife through his chest. Yu pitied the god and buried him. After that this place was called the State of Penetrating the Chest.

It seems that dragons liked to help emperors, sages and worthies. The primary way for them was to become mounts for these individuals. An infinitely resourceful Taoist immortal named Hu Gong went to the fairy land with a friend called Fei Zhangfang. Later on, because Fei Zhangfang missed his home, Hu Gong let him ride his stick to return there. After riding the stick for awhile, Fei Zhangfang felt sleepy. When he opened his eyes, he saw the gate of his home. Then he threw the stick into the valley and it turned into a green dragon. From this story, we can see that the relation between the dragon and Taoism was close, sometimes intimate. In *Account of the Saints*, a person named Zi Ming went angling by a stream. He happened to catch the son of the white dragon. Because Zi Ming was a kind person, he let the son go. Later he caught a white fish with a letter inside its belly. The contents of the letter taught Zi Ming how to become an immortal. Three years later, the white dragon sent him to the White Dragon Mountain. Zi Ming lived more than one hundred years on this mountain.

More fantastic was the combination of dragon stories with medicine, divination, and similar arts from other countries. According to *The Book of Master Bao Pu*, there was a wizard in the Western Regions. He puffed air into water and a dragon emerged. It was several dozen meters long. As the wizard continued to puff air, the dragon became shorter until it was only ten-odd centimeters in length. The wizard then put it into a bottle of water. Wherever a drought occurred, the wizard would went to the area to rent the skills of his dragon. After collecting money, he would put the dragon into a pool and blow on it. The dragon would become bigger and bigger until it was several hundred meters long. Not long afterward, it would rain in the drought area.

This story of a dragon bringing rain did not originate in the Western Regions. In *The Book of the Prince of Huainan* of the Han Dynasty, it is said that whenever a dragon came, clouds would appear. This was known by the phrase "cloud follows the dragon." So the cloud and the dragon complemented each other. Because rain comes from clouds, people thought the dragon could bring rain. A story from *Journey to the West* illustrates this point. The Dragon King of the East Sea transformed himself into a man and walked into the market. He saw a fortune-teller there predicting how much it would rain at certain time the next day. The Dragon King of the East Sea thought this was ridiculous, and he didn't even know how much it would rain the next day although he was in charge of the rain. He told the fortune-teller that he doubted the prediction and made a bet with the man. To the Dragon King's surprise, he received an imperial edict from the Heaven God when he returned to his palace. The Heaven God told him to rain a certain number of drops at certain time the next day. What the edict demanded was exactly the same amount that the fortune-teller had predicted. The Dragon King, however, didn't want to admit defeat, and so he rained several less drops. Then he went to see the fortune-teller. The fortune-teller laughed grimly: "Do you realize that you've committed a major crime?" Not long afterward the Dragon King of the East Sea was sentenced to death for disobeying an imperial edict. He had to ask for the fortune-teller what to do. The fortune-teller told the Dragon King of the East Sea to escape because the executor was to be Prime Minister Wei Zheng. The Dragon King of the East Sea did so, but Wei Zheng still dreamed of killing him. This story of the Dragon King of the East Sea has been humanized in various literary works.

There is an idiom relating to the relationship between the dragon and rain. It is "a carp jumps over the dragon gate," and it comes from the fact that the Yellow River flows by Mount Longmen where the current is swift. In late spring carp swim here against the current. If one of them is able to jump over the dragon gate it will become a dragon. It was said that clouds and rain would follow it and heaven fire would burn its tail if a carp went over the dragon gate. This shows that the dragon, cloud and rain are related to each other, and this idiom points to a person who achieves a meteoric rise in social status.

Of the other idioms related to a dragon, we'd like to introduce "bring a picture of a dragon to life by putting in the pupils of its eyes." This comes from a story concerning art. A painter during the Tang Dynasty named Zhang Sengyao painted dragons for a temple. He painted four dragons without any eyes, saying that the dragons would fly if he put in the pupils of their eyes. Some people didn't believe him and asked him to add the eyes. So he put in the pupils for two of the dragons' eyes. Not long afterward, thunder and lightning destroyed the wall and the two dragons rose into the air. Only the two without eyes remained. This ancient story is well known among Chinese artists. It indicates that each work should have its most touching part.

In conclusion, we will tell a fable known even to children in China. It is called "Lord Ye's Love of Dragons." A person named Ye Zigao loved dragons and painted and carved many of them in his room. The Heaven Dragon was moved by this devotion and visited him. When the dragon put its head in the window, Ye was so frightened he was scared out of his wits. Today, we use this idiom to satirize one who does not like what he pretends to like.

6. Snake

Among the twelve zodiac animals, the snake follows the dragon. Its body is similar in shape to that of a dragon, and so people also call it a little dragon. In ancient Chinese documents, the dragon and snake always went together in such phrases as "flying dragon rides on a cloud, rising snake swims on mist." No wonder some regarded the snake as the origin of the dragon. In popular culture, people liked to lump the dragon and snake together. For instance, in the lower reaches of the Yangtze River people had the custom of feeding domestic snakes that they called green dragons. There was a snake island in northeast China where the many Pallas pit vipers were called little dragon kings by the people who lived there. Some people even thought that the dragon was the remains of a dead snake. A folk song in Hunan Province goes: "Southern snakes will become dragons after shedding their skins." This was a long-standing belief that the dragon and snake were the same thing. A scholar of Tang Dynasty, Yan Shigu, told this story. One day the sky was covered with dark clouds and thunder roared. Two boys in red and two boys in green arrived at the major hall of a temple. They removed a three-meter long white snake from one column and a six-meter long white snake from another column, saying that the two columns were hollow and that is where the dragons hid. Here the dragons are indicated by two white snakes. According to *Notes Written in a Dream* by the scholar of Song Dynasty, Shen Kuo, a little snake climbed into a boat and the boatman called it "little dragon of Pengze Lake." It seems that the only difference between a dragon and a snake lies in their sizes. But there was a huge snake in one fairy tale. It was said that there was a mountain northwest of Kunlun Mountain, which was 15,000 km in circumference. The snake that encircled the mountain was 45,000 km long. It lived in the mountain and ate in the sea. This snake was equal in size to a dragon, and maybe it was a dragon.

Certainly, according to biology, a snake is a snake with its own habits and characteristics, while a dragon is an imaginary animal.

The snake in fairy tales is strange and beyond all expectations. Many of them and the characteristics they have cannot be found in nature.

According to an ancient Chinese legend, there was a snake mountain in the East Sea. The terrain was strategically situated, difficult to access and damp. Many snakes with human heads lived on the mountain. In Chinese fairy tales there were often people with snake bodies, most of whom were females such as Nüwa, the creator-goddess of the Chinese nation. Maybe the snake belonged to the *yin* category as do females, the earth, rain and harvests, so it was worshipped for its reproductive capabilities. *The Book of Songs* says that the snake is a "good omen for women." So the description of a snake with a human head in this fairy tale has a certain symbolic meaning.

According to the *Records of Mount Guzhu*, there was a kind of tree-climbing snake that lived in an ochre cave. With a length of one meter, it liked to hang on the branches of the trees and fly away whenever it saw people. In *Brief Record of Contemporary News*, there was a revenge snake in the south of the Five Regions.

It would follow you as far as 2,500 meters if you touched it. If one was killed by some person, hundreds of other snakes would gather. The way to protect oneself from this kind of snake was to carry a centipede. Another story was told about a yellow throated snake. Living on a roof, it was not harmful to people, but instead ate other poisonous snakes. After it was full, it would look down from the roof and foam at the mouth. If the foam spurted out, the foam would turn into sand insects. People would get sick if they touched such insects.

Classic of Mountains and Rivers speaks of a kind of snake on Mount Taihua, which had six feet and two wings. In *Records of the Investigation of Things*, there listed a kind of snake that could swallow an elephant and spit out the bones three years later. And *The Miscellany of the Youyang Mountains* mentions a kind of river snake in Nan'an that came out of the water between May and June. After the first big snake landed, countless other snakes would follow it to the area where people lived.

There is a description of a cockscomb snake which had a head that was similar to that of a cock. It lived on Mount Huiji. People would die immediately after the snake bit them. And another snake which was gray and less than one meter long, would fly from the forest after hearing people's voice. People whoever was assaulted by it would die immediately. There was a yellow necked snake living in a stone crack. Whenever it rained, the snake would roar like ox. People would die if they heard its voice.

All the above were strange members of the snake family and justified the fear that humans had of snakes. But in many stories and fairy tales, the image of snake is not terrible at all.

We earlier mentioned the story of the King of Qin opening a road in Sichuan Province with the help of five strong men. There is another tale about this king that concerns a snake. The King of Qin sent five beautiful women to the King of Shu as a gift. The King of Shu sent five strong men to meet the women and escort them to his palace. When they arrived at Zitong, the group saw a big snake entering a cave. One strong man wanted to pull it out by holding onto its tail. But he failed, even though the other four people helped him. Instead, the mountain crashed. All five strong men and the five beauties died. The crashed mountain was separated into five ridges on one of which lay a big flat stone. The King of Shu felt sad when he heard the news of their deaths. He built a missing-wife terrace on the flat stone and named this ridge the five-beauty tomb mountain. People in later generations also called it the five-man tomb.

In the *New Writings* by Jia Yi of the Han Dynasty, there is this story: When Sun Shuao was young, he once went out to play. After he came back home, he felt heavyhearted and ate nothing. His mother asked him what had happened. He cried that he couldn't live any longer because he had met a snake with two heads and people said one would die if they met a two-headed snake. His mother asked him where the snake was. Sun Shuao said that he had killed it for he did not want others to see it and also die. The mother comforted him, saying, "Don't worry. I have heard that God will bless people with virtues. You've done a good thing. God will bless you." Obviously, this story of snake is told to praise of the spirit of sacrifice.

In reality, the snake has always been somewhat of a danger to humans but a snake can build a friendly relationship with people in fairy tales. This close relation between humans and snakes can be found in the tales of mystery and the supernatural of the Jin and Northern and Southern dynasties. According to the *Stories of Immortals*, Dou Wu's mother bore a snake when giving birth to him. His mother let the snake go back into the forest instead of killing it. When his mother died, a big snake appeared at the funeral out of the grass. Its head knocked on the coffin and it shed tears and blood and had a sorrowful look. Other people knew that this was the little snake paying its debt of gratitude. Another story in this same book says that a duke of Sui cured a wounded snake on one of his travels. Later, the snake held jewelry in its mouth to present to the duke of Sui. The idiom "Sui jewelry" comes from this story. It indicates that one must pay a debt of gratitude when one becomes aware of it.

The folk story that particularly expresses the close relation between snakes and humans is *The Tale of the White Snake*. It is said that in 807 A.D. a white lady visited West Lake with her servant girl, Xiaoqing. There, by chance, she met a young scholar named Xu Xian. They fell in love at first sight and were married. They had a son by their marriage. One day Xu Xian was frightened when he found that the white lady and Xiaoqing were really snakes. But he didn't want to disclose the truth because of his love for the white lady, and so they still lived as husband and wife. But eventually his family members discovered the truth and asked the Master of the Law to exercise some magic. Then the white lady and Xiaoqing were put into a jar which was placed under Leifeng Tower forever. After that, Xu Xian was deep in sorrow because he missed his beloved wife. There are many fairy tales related to this story. It was a matter of mystery and the supernatural at first, but gradually the tales began to focus on the love tragedy between the hero and heroin. At the same time, people have shown great sympathy for the white lady—the snake. Maybe this is the most humanized image of a snake in traditional Chinese culture.

The turning of a snake into a human can be often found in Chinese fairy tales. Instead of being a romantic happening, as in the tale of the white lady, most of these stories are bizarre. In *New Anecdotes of Social Talk*, a famous general of the Jin Dynasty, Du Yu, once became drunk at a banquet and went back to his room, which he locked tightly. A low-ranking official looked into the room through the window when he heard the sound of vomiting. He saw nobody there but there was a snake vomiting. It was Du Yu revealing his true snake body after he became drunk.

Besides turning into humans, there were other unusual relations between snakes and humans such as the snake's ability to make predictions and to point to symbolic meanings. According to *Notes on Social Customs*, an officer named Feng Gun opened a box one day which was packed with ribbons. He was shocked when he found a one meter long red snake moving from south to north among the ribbons. A fortune-teller later told him this was an auspicious sign. It meant that he would be a frontier general in the east. Five years later, Feng Gun was appointed as General-in-Chief and Governor of Liaodong. Another story is related to the names of the 12 zodiac animals. A scholar of the Song Dynasty found a little snake in his room. The snake appeared during *sishi* the period of the day from 9 a.m. to 11 a.m. and vanished at *wushi* the period of the day from 11 a.m. to 1 p.m. When the snake reappeared, he put it into an iron cage. At *wushi* the snake turned into a vivid and elegant stone figure. At *sishi* the next day, the snake began to move, and it became stone again at *wushi*. This happened every day. In the twelve Earthly Branches, or twelve two-hour periods, the snake is at the position of *si*, so it only had life at this period. At other times, it became a work of stone art. Obviously, this story points to the meaning of the zodiac animals.

Lastly, let's talk about two quotations relating to the snake. One is "the snake of Mount Changshan." Coming from *Master Sun's Art of War*, it indicates that one should give consideration to both the head and the tail when using military forces, just like the snake of Mount Changshan. When one attacked its head, its tail would help; when the tail was attacked, its head would help; when its belly was under attack, both its head and tail would aid together. The other quotation is from *Records of the Warring States*, and is "draw a snake and add feet to it." Several people were together but had only one cup of wine. They didn't know how to decide who should drink it. So they agreed to each draw a picture of snake on the ground, and the person who finished first would get to drink the wine. One person finished quickly and took the cup, but then he said, "I can add feet to it." He continued the drawing, adding feet to the snake. Then before he finished, another person completed his drawing and took away the cup, saying, "A snake has no feet at all. So you don't need to add them to it." This man drained the cup. This story warns people not to ruin an effect by adding something superfluous.

7. Horse

The horse, as well as ox, has played an important role in the progress of human society. It is difficult to imagine what Chinese history would have been like without it. At least it would not have been as grand and magnificent as it is now. Therefore, the horse occupies a decisive position in Chinese history and it was involved in many important historic events. Moreover, it was one of the crucial factors that had determined the outcome of war. Many of the most famous generals made their illustrious names known by using their horses. Therefore, the horse first established its reputation on the battle field. For example, the steed of Xiang Yu (a leader of peasant forces during the third century B.C.), went bravely on expeditions with Xiang Yu. When Xiang Yu was surrounded by enemies and caught in a hopeless situation at Gaixia, his final thoughts lay with his horse. He gave it to a neighborhood head near Wujiang River before his death, saying, "This horse has followed me for five years. Riding it, I advanced at a tremendous pace, and it has been invincible. Now that my last day has come, I cannot bear to see it killed. So I would like give it to you." He then looked up at the sky and drew a deep sigh. "I am an earth-shaking hero of the age, but Heaven does not help me, and my horse can no longer follow me." Then he cut his throat with his sword by the side of the Wujiang River. Later generations would think of his battle steed, whenever they mentioning the name of Xiang Yu.

Loyal and devoted to their owners, the battle steeds went through fire and danger with them, and often saved their owners from calamity. This close relationship between the horses and their owners has been significant throughout history. When Liu Bei first got his steed, he was told that it might hurt him, but he wouldn't believe this. Once Liu Bei went to meet Liu Biao, the magistrate of Xiangyang. There he discovered that the subordinates of Liu Biao plotted to murder him, so he rode his horse to flee. The horse became stuck in mud and could not move when Liu Bei tried to cross Tanshuixi Lake. Meanwhile the pursuing troops were drawing closer. In a moment of desperation, Liu Bei said to his horse, "Now I am caught in a hopeless situation, can you make further efforts to save me?" As if understanding his words, the horse sprang with all its might nearly ten meters high, and reached the opposite bank. Thus Liu Bei escaped from death. Since then, this story has been passed down with approval as a part of war history. However, the major character is not the hero Liu Bei, but his steed.

There are many such examples in the historic records and folk legends that show a horse's function and position in war. At the same time, a horse was even more important to people who went on expeditions all year around. War frequently broke out in ancient China, especially during the earliest ages, when warlike monarchs were common and most of them had excellent horses. These were an important means by which to win the battles at that time. According to the *Records of the Historian*, hearing that there was a magnificent horse in the State of Dawan in the Western Regions. Emperor Wu Di of Han sent his men there to ask for the horse and to bring money and local excellent horses as a gift to the monarch of the State of Dawan. The emperor was very anxious to obtain this horse. The monarch of the State of Dawan accepted the money and presents, but would not give up the horse. Irritated, the envoy returned to report this to the emperor, who flew into a rage, and ordered Li Guangli, the commanding general, to send armed forces to suppress the Dawan State. Thus an unprecedentedly cruel war broke out. Of course, fighting for a horse should not be approved. However, from this story, we can see how people valued horses in that age.

Since the horse was regarded as so important that there were people who made a profession of judging the worth of horses. Such persons were necessary, otherwise how could people tell whether a horse was excellent or not? Of course, a horse's ability could only be finally determined by its involvement in war or other activities.

However, it was undoubtedly necessary to observe a horse's properties beforehand as a guarantee for war or other activities. Therefore, the skill of judging horses according to their appearance appeared in the ancient China when the horse was particularly valued, and a number of masters in this field of judging emerged. Among these judges Bo Le was most famous. In fact, the meaning of the name Bo Le in traditional culture went far beyond just telling excellent horses from average ones. The name came to symbolize a person with discerning eyes who could discover qualified personnel. However, Bo Le's experiences become the guidance to all who judge horses in later generations. The *Scripture for Judging a Horse* recorded Bo Le's methods. For example, he believed that the three kinds of weak horses and the five kinds of inferior ones should be eliminated first. The three weak varieties included horses with large heads and small necks; soft backs and large abdomens; and small necks and large hoofs. The five inferior ones included horses with large heads and flat ears; long but not curved necks; short upper parts and long lower parts of the body; large skeletons and short ribs; shallow hips and thin thighs. These methods have now become a part of the knowledge of veterinary medicine, and most horses are now used in agriculture and animal husbandry. In ancient times, the ox was mainly used in agricultural production, while the horse was mainly used in war. As we know, ancient China was an agricultural nation (as China still is), while the successive dynasties and social changes were mostly prompted by war. Therefore, the ox and the horse became the two wheels of China's historic development.

Of course, the horse is not only a useful tool in war, and its functions are not restricted to war. We can find many wonderful things about a horse, including its wide variety and relevant characteristics.

According to the *History of the Han Dynasty*, the aforementioned Dawan horse in Dawan State would sweat blood when it was running, and it became an important symbol for judging horses. Another book also records that there was a horse in Dawanqiu with a total length of over six meters. It could run a thousand *li* in a single day, and would sweat blood at noon. Riders had to wrap their heads, waists and abdomen with silk. So we can see that the Dawan horse was considered the best in ancient times. Otherwise the Emperor Wu Di of Han would not have launched a war to get it. There are many ancient poems that praise the Dawan horse, for example, Du Fu's verse, "The famous horse in the Western Regions named the Dawan horse."

Various magical horses were also recorded in ancient books. In one ancient book it is said that there was a horse yellow in color and shaped like a fox, with two horns on its back. Anyone who rode it could live as long as three thousand years. Some people believe that the magical horse might have been a gnu. Another ancient classic records a magical horse with red mouth and black body.

The ancient people liked to give horses beautiful names according to their appearance and characteristics. The description "winged steed," for example, not only refers to horses which can run quick enough to a thousand *li* a day, but also may refer to people with outstanding abilities. For the ancient monarchs, their love for winged steeds became a symbol for their seeking out of able men. A monarch during the Warring States Period posted a notice to solicit the service of the virtuous and capable, announcing that anyone who offered a "winged steed" would be awarded 500 *liang* of gold. Our man presented a horse's skeleton, saying that it was the remains of a winged steed. The monarch became angry. He said what he wanted was a live horse, not its remains. The offerer replied that if people saw that the monarch was even receiving the bones of a winged steed, they would understand he really thirsted after talent, and all able men would come to him voluntarily. The monarch saw the logic of this argument and nodded his approval. He awarded the man 500 *liang* of gold. As expected, when this news spread, talented people from everywhere came. It is a pity that there were few monarchs who were so fond of talented people. Thus Han Yu, a writer in the Tang Dynasty, sighed with feeling, "winged steeds are available, yet we lack Bo Le."

In the legends, the horse and the dragon have a close relationship. The horse that pulled the carriage for an emperor was often called a "dragon" because the dragon symbolized the emperor in the ancient times. In the *Journey to the West*, Monk Tang Seng's white horse was originally a dragon, symbolizing its honorable status.

There is a legend about the relationship between a horse and a silkworm. According to this legend, in remote antiquity there was a girl who missed her father because he was away on an expedition. She told her horse that if it could bring her father back, she would marry it. The horse then departed and returned carrying her father. After that, the horse became quite excited whenever it saw the girl. When her father learned the reason for this, he killed the horse, and dried its skin in the courtyard. One day while the girl was playing on the horse's skin, it suddenly wrapped around her and flew away. Later, people found the horse skin hanging on a big tree. The girl had turned into a silkworm. To commemorate this event, later generations called the silkworm a "horse-headed lady," and there are statues of a woman with horse skin draping over her shoulders in some local temples. She is regarded as the silkworm goddess.

Many ancient artists were fond of painting horses, and some of them, such as Han Gan, a painter during the Tang Dynasty, were specially famous for painting them. The imperial art academy also often asked examinees to paint horses. For example, one famous examination topic of the imperial art academy during the Song Dynasty was for students to depict the verse "after admiring flowers, the horse's hoofs became fragrant." Most of the examinees painted bees flying around a horse's hoofs to express the fragrance of the flowers.

8. Sheep

The sheep is a relatively meek animal. Therefore, it is regarded as a symbol of virtue and morals, and for this reason it is often used in sacrificial rites. According to the *Luxuriant Dew of the Spring and Autumn Annals*, the sheep has horns but is not bellicose, as if it is benevolent; it does not cry when it is caught, and does not resent it when it is killed, as if it is righteous; and lambs kneel down to suck milk, as if they are particularly polite. Therefore, the sheep symbolizes good luck, and can be offered as a present. But sheep should first be offered respectfully to ancestors and gods, i.e., used in sacrificial rites. As recorded in the *Rites of the Zhou Dynasty*, there were people who were specially designated to use sheep in sacrificial rites. They would cut off the sheep's heads and use them as offerings at that time. This sounds cruel, yet because courtesy was regarded as the most important virtue in the ancient China, it was believed to be fair and reasonable to sacrifice sheep. Even Confucius, when hearing someone reproaching the treatment of sheep as sacrificial offerings, said that that person loved sheep, while he loved courtesy. Therefore, it was unavoidable for a sheep to sacrifice itself for courtesy.

In addition, sheep is a delicious food, which could be served to guests. The Chinese character meaning "beautiful" consists of a top part which, by itself, means "sheep" and a bottom part which means "big." The character for "sheep" is also found in many other positive words, so the sheep may symbolize beauty and good fortune. The city of Guangzhou is also sometimes called Yangcheng (Sheep City). According to a legend, five immortals descended into the city of Guangzhou riding five sheep of different colors, and brought an ear of grain (*sui*) from the celestial valley to the local people so as to bring them good luck. (Therefore Guangzhou is also sometimes called Sui). The statues of the five sheep are now standing in Yuexiu Park in the city of Guangzhou.

Because sheep symbolize good luck, the ancient people believed that a jade sheep would appear when the world became peaceful and auspicious; and if anyone saw a jade sheep, they would live happily ever after. It is said that during the Warring States Period, Duke Ai of Lu asked the people to dig a well. They dug for three months, but no water appeared. Instead, they found a jade sheep. Duke Ai of Lu decided this was an omen of good luck and ordered the people to sing and dance in celebration. The jade sheep lived underground, so it must have been a magical sheep. However, the magical sheep in legends were not limited to jade sheep. It is said that, Yu Liang, an official during the period of Yongming of the Southern Qi, heard the sound of bleating in his bedroom, and suspected that it came from a god or spirit. He looked through the window and saw a sheep with the height of almost one meter and red hair, whose radiance brightened the whole room. There is another magical sheep mentioned in this work that had a single horn and could settle lawsuits. Crime suspects were brought to this sheep and if it touched them, they were guilty, if not, they were innocent. It is said that this method was used by a great judge, named Ao Tao, in ancient times. The ancients believed that a sheep with single horn was an incarnation of a dragon, and that it should not be killed. If it was, the man who killed it would die.

Jade sheep and other magical sheep are, of course, only legends, and there are all sorts of other strange sheep in fairy tales and legends, including sheep gods and ghosts. The *Stories of Immortals* records a famous tale about Zong Dingbo catching a ghost. One day when Zong Dingbo was walking alone when he suddenly met a ghost. The ghost asked him who he was, and Zong said that he was also a ghost. So the two of them walked together. After a while, they felt tired. The ghost suggested that they carry one another on their backs while walking. Zong did not feel any weight when he carried the ghost, while the ghost found Zong quite heavy and asked him the reason. Zong replied that he was a new ghost, and then asked what thing the ghost most feared. The ghost told him that it was to be spat upon by people. At dawn, Zong Dingbo grabbed the ghost and held it tightly until the ghost revealed its original shape. It was a sheep. Fearing that the sheep might change back into a ghost again. Zong Dingbo spat on him, and then sold the sheep in the market. This story was also collected in *Strange Tales from a Make Do Studio*, a famous short-story collection written by Pu Songling, a novelist during the Qing Dynasty.

It is said that a sheep's most distinguishing characteristic was its ability to change its shape, and it most easily turned into stone. A story is told that when one of China's most famous craftsmen built the Zhaozhou Bridge, he asked the stones on the mountain to change into sheep so that he could drive them to the construction site, and then he asked them to change back into stones. Thus the bridge was built. As the *Tale of Immortals* records, a young man named Huang Chuping, while herding sheep, went to Jinghua Mountain with a Taoist priest and did not return for several years. His brother looked for him everywhere. At last, the brother met the Taoist priest, and asked him where the sheep herder was. The priest arranged for the two brothers meet each other. The elder one asked where the sheep were, and so his younger one led him to see them. But what he saw were many white stones. Then the younger brother shouted loudly at the stones, "stand up, sheep!" The white stones stood up, and turned into tens of thousands of sheep.

Besides changing into stones, sheep could also turn into fish. There is a place named Yanglongtan in Yunnan, the name of which originated from a story about sheep changing into fish. According to this legend, when a young herdsman was taking care of sheep by the river, the dragon king's daughter suddenly appeared and invited him to go to the dragon's palace at the bottom of the river. The young man agreed to do so and drove his sheep into the water as he followed her. The sheep turned into fish as soon as they entered the water.

In such fairy tales, the sheep had many mysterious characteristics, and thus many intriguing stories came into being. As recorded in the *Stories of Ghosts and Men*, a vicious woman wanted to murder her husband and so she hit him over the head and pushed him into a cave. After a long while, he came to. Within the cave he saw a palace decorated with dazzling jewelry. A huge giant led him around the palace so that he could visit the place. They visited nine rooms before the man began to feel hungry. So the giant pointed to a sheep and told the man to stroke its beard. The sheep spat out a pear which the man ate to satisfy his hunger. He felt so happy that he wanted to stay there, but the giant wouldn't let him.

Some strange tales about sheep stress the relationship between sheep and humans. As we know, the sheep is a relatively meek animal, and people like to show its kind natural characteristics through fairy tales. According to the *Tale of Immortals*, when a man named Zuo Ci was being pursued, he ran among a large group of sheep and disappeared. The pursuer suspected that he had changed to a sheep, and so the man ordered that they be counted. The sheep originally numbered 1,000, but now there was one more. The pursuer then knew that Zuo Ci had really turned into a sheep. He ordered the sheep into which Zuo Ci had transformed himself to stand out. The man promised that he would do him no harm. A sheep walked forward and knelt down, saying "What do you want?" The pursuer started to catch the sheep. However, at that moment, all the other sheep knelt down and said, "What do you want?" Deeply moved, the pursuer gave up his investigation, and departed. The story shows the chivalrous attitude sheep have for humans.

In the various tales sheep were always friendly towards people, and they understood human nature. However, if a person refused to save a dying sheep, it would revenge itself on him. As recorded in the *Sequel to Stories of Immortals*, a rich man entertained some guests, including a monk. He was about to kill a sheep to treat the guests, when the sheep struggled to free itself from the rope and hid under the monk's cloak for protection. But the monk remained indifferent to it, and so the sheep was finally killed and cooked. The rich man asked the monk to taste the mutton first. The monk put a piece into his mouth, but before he could swallow it, the mutton entered into his skin. The monk felt a great pain, and asked for treatment but nothing that was tried had any effect on him. He had no choice but to tear his skin away so as to take out the mutton. He became ill after that, and would often bleat like a sheep. The monk died soon afterward. The story is told in a very sentimental way. It is said that sheep would kneel down and cry before being killed, and therefore it was cruel to kill one.

There are other strange sheep in fairy tales, such as a sheep that was as large as a donkey, a flying sheep that pulled a cart for an immortal, a sheep with a green tail, and a *yuezhi* large-tailed sheep with a tail that would always grow out after it was cut off. All these have added mysterious dimensions to the sheep of the Chinese zodiac.

9. Monkey

Although the sheep could change its shape, the animal that could do this best was the monkey. In the *Journey to the West*, the most outstanding skill of Sun Wukong, one of the most popular monkey figures in Chinese literature, was that he could change into 72 different shapes by which he defeated various demons and escorted Sanzang, Tang Priest to the West safely. In the earlier fairy tales and legends, there were many monkeys who were good at changing shape. Thus this skill of the monkey gave rise to a number of strange tales.

Probably, because of the blood relationship between the monkey and human beings, the monkey usually changed into a man in fairy tales. The ancients believed that the monkey had a natural instinct for changing into a man. This can be seen by the idiom "a monkey with a hat on," which means to dress up a monkey trying to fool people into believing that it is a man. As recorded in *The Book of Master Bao Pu*, a monkey would turn into an old man if it lived to be 1,000 years of age. A story from *On the Supplement of Omissions* tells that when Zhou Qun, a scholar during the Three Kingdoms Period, was gathering medicine on Minshan Mountain, he saw a white monkey come down from the peak and stand before him. He was about to stab it with his sword when the monkey suddenly turned into an old man and handed him a jade plate. Zhou Qun was so surprised that he asked the old man when he was born. The old man said that he could not remember, but only the history since Xuan Yuan, an alternative name of Huang Di (emperor), regarded as the first great ruler of China. This story shows that a monkey could become an old man if it lived to 1,000 years in age.

However, in the fairy tales, monkeys did not need to wait 1,000 years to become men. Many of them could change suddenly into humans, and then change just as quickly back into monkeys. It is said that a young woman in the state of Yue during the Warring States Period was quite skillful at swordsmanship. One day she met an old man called himself Yuan Gong. The man said to the woman, "It is said that you are good at flourishing shores. Can you show this to me?" The woman said, "It's no secret. We can have a competition." So they broke two branches off a tree to have a contest. After several rounds, the old man sprang up into a tree, and changed into a white monkey. The old man turned out to be a monkey.

Sun Wukong escorted Sanzang, Tang Priest to go on his pilgrimage to the West to obtain Buddhist scriptures. He used his skill by changing into 72 different shapes to protect his master. Few monkeys in other fairy tales had such lofty motivations. One of their "sinister" intentions was to seduce or capture women. According to *More Stories of Immortals*, a duke named Zhai Zhao during the Jin Dynasty raised a monkey in his harem. After some time, two of the maids became pregnant at the same time, and gave birth to three children who could spring as soon as they were born. Zhai Zhao realized that the monkey was the troublemaker. Irritated, he killed the monkey and the children. The two maids cried loudly, saying that they had seen a lovely young man wearing a yellow coat who had the same manner as any man. Obviously, this young man in yellow was the changed monkey.

There were also some monkeys living deep in the mountains who sometimes came down to capture women. *Stories of Immortals* says that an animal living on a high mountain in southwest Sichuan was like monkey, but its height was over two meters and could walk as a man. It was called either Jiaguo or Mahua. It often hid by the roadside, and sneaked to attack a passing woman. When it captured one, it brought the young woman back to its home in the mountains. The animal could tell women from men by their smell and it could determine this at a long distance. It caught women by a long rope, and would make any captured woman its wife. She would, however, be sent back home with her child after giving birth. The child was the same as an ordinary child and its family name was Yang. Therefore, Yang was the family name for the most of the local people, and most of them were the off springs of Jiaguo or Mahua. Although this story described people with specific names in a particular place, it was only a fairy tale, and no one living in southwest Sichuan would ever admit that they were the off springs of this animal. But such tales may be related to the affinity between men and monkeys in the evolutionary history of human beings. Probably there were few men at the place that the monkeys took the responsibility for their reproduction. However, the story itself shows a monkey's habits and characteristics in capturing women to satisfy its lust.

The *Tale of a White Ape*, a well-known short story from the Tang Dynasty, describes an ape that captures men's wives. During the Chen Dynasty of the Southern Dynasties (557-589 A.D.), a general named Ouyang He led his troops through a pass deep in the mountains. His wife was with him. A subordinate told him that there was a local demon who would capture beautiful women if it could. Hearing this, Ouyang He took careful precautions. He hid his wife in a heavily-guarded secret room at night. Late one night, a sinister wind blew with great force and there was utter darkness. The guards were all asleep. Ouyang He was suddenly awakened, and he found that his wife had disappeared. He was very sad, and ordered his soldiers to look for her at daybreak. After a month, one of his wife's embroidered shoes was found over 100 *li* from their camping site. Another ten-odd days passed before the searchers discovered a cave in a mountain over 200 *li* away. There were dozens of women in the cave, and Ouyang He learned that they had been captured by a demon with extraordinary great strength and outstanding fighting skills. He asked the women where his wife was, and they told him that she was ill in bed. After finding his wife in the cave, Ouyang He decided to catch the demon. A dozens days later, the demon returned. The women entertained him, and made him drunk. Ouyang He then led the troops into the cave and caught the demon. It was a huge white ape. Ouyang He killed it, and brought his wife home. Soon afterward, his wife gave birth to a son, who looked exactly like an ape when he grew up. This was Ouyang Xun, a famous calligrapher during the early Tang Dynasty. It is said that because Ouyang Xun looked like a monkey, someone invented this story to make fun of him. The story was based on a monkey's natural instincts as described in the legends about capturing women to satisfy its lust. As early as the Han Dynasty, one scholar wrote in his book that a big monkey on Nanshan Mountain had stolen his beautiful wife. People therefore got the impression that monkeys have a desire to capture men's wives to satisfy their lust.

Of course there are other legends about monkeys, and some of them are quite moving. The ballad titled "The Wail of a Monkey Is So Touching That it Makes People Cry," which is sung in the Three Gorges area of the Yangtze River is a touching tale about a monkey. According to the legend behind this ballad, soldiers caught a little monkey on the bank of the river, when they passed through the Three Gorges, and they brought it onto the ship. After a while, the mother monkey appeared on the bank. She followed the ship wailing sadly. When the ship drew close to the bank, the mother monkey jumped onto it and died immediately afterward. The soldiers cut her abdomen open, and found that her intestines were broken into pieces because of her sadness. The word "heartbroken," which is now often used to describe sadness may have originated from this story.

There are also some other interesting stories relating to monkeys. A story tells that a man raising monkeys fed them acorn nuts. He told them he would give each monkey three nuts in the morning, and four in the evening. The monkeys were quite angry at this. So he said that he would give each of them four in the morning, and three in the evening. Thinking they had won a small advantage, the monkeys gladly agreed. At first this story was used to show how a man could hoodwink monkeys, but later it became a metaphor to describe people's changeableness. From the story, we can see that bright monkeys can sometimes be fooled, and we can also imagine their charmingly naive manners.

10. Rooster

Because a rooster has wings, the ancients classified it as a "bird," and mentioned it in the same breath with a phoenix, crane or wild goose. Probably a rooster in the remote antiquity could fly, while nowadays it can only flop in the air for a second, and can hardly leave the ground. Therefore, it is a two-footed animal walking on the ground.

The most impressive characteristic of a rooster is that it announces the arrival of dawn by crowing, while hens can only cackle. Therefore people often associate a rooster with the sun. It is said that there was a three-footed bird in the sun which was believed a rooster. According to the principles of *yin* and *yang*, the rooster is a collection of *yang*, and the sun is the spirit of *yang*. The two belong to the same category, and for this reason, the rooster crows when the sun rises, indicating their interaction. In reality, a rooster's crowing reports the arrival of a new day. There is a fairy tale about this. It is said that there was a huge tree with 1,500-kilometer-long branches named Taodu on Taodu Mountain in the southeast. On it stood a heavenly rooster. The rooster would crow as soon as the sunshine brightened the tree branches, and all the other roosters in the world would follow it. Legend also has it that a jade rooster once lived on Fusang Mountain in the east that would crow as soon as the sun rose. A golden rooster would follow this, then the stone rooster, and finally all the other roosters in the world would begin to crow successively.

There is also a famous story about a rooster's crow in the

Records of the Historian written by Sima Qian. According to this story, Prince Meng Chang of Qi during the Warring States Period made friends extensively, including with all sorts of hangers-on and even thieves. Others sneered at him for making friends with such humble men, but he believed there was nothing wrong with doing so. Once he encountered danger when he was leading a group of his hangers-on to visit Qin. It was before daybreak when they fled to the Hangu Pass, but the guards wouldn't open the gate until a rooster crowed. One of the hangers-on, who could imitate a rooster's crow, gave out such a sound, and roosters everywhere followed suit. The soldiers therefore opened the gate, and thus Prince Meng Chang escaped.

Besides its practical uses, the rooster is also linked to various virtues. It is said that its crest symbolizes gentleness; its feet, which can be used to wrestle with great power and energy, tremendous courage; its willingness to share food with companions, humanity; and its always announcing the arrival of dawn on time, trustworthiness. Therefore, the rooster is regarded as a noble animal, and it could be used for sacrificial rites. However, roosters are generally unwilling to accept such a courteous reception. According to the *Zuo Qiuming's Commentary on the Spring and Autumn Annals*, someone saw a large rooster break its tail in the countryside near a city and asked his servant the reason for this. The servant replied that the rooster did this out of fear of becoming a victim in a sacrificial rite.

Cockfighting was a popular entertainment in ancient China, loved by both the common people and emperors. It is said that King Xuan of Zhou was fond of cockfighting, and a man named Ji Xiaozi was put specially in charge of raising gamecocks for him. However, the most famous "cockfighting-loving emperor" was Emperor Xuan Zong of Tang Dynasty. A story wrote by novelist Chen Hong of the Tang Dynasty, Emperor Xuan Zong loved to view cockfights in the Festival of Pure Brightness before he ascended the throne. After coming to power, he established a department to raise gamecocks. He kept the most excellent ones gathered from Chang'an City, and gathered some rascals together to raise and train them. Cockfighting became popular throughout the whole country at that time; many people wished that they could master the art or offer excellent gamecocks to the emperor so that they would win wealth and rank. There was a young man named Jia Zhang who became wealthy and powerful because of this. The story by Chen Hong tells about Jia Zhang's rise to power and position and his later decline. Emperor Xuan Zong led a luxurious and dissipated life, and as a result, he soon lost his country and throne. Cockfighting was the leading factor in Emperor Xuan Zong's tragic fate.

Interestingly, it is said that Emperor Xuan Zong was fond of cockfighting because he was born in the year of the rooster. it seems that the emperors born in the year of the rooster had a special love for the animal. What is more interesting is the fact that Emperor Ren Zong of the Yuan Dynasty forbade people living in Dadu City (now Beijing) to carry roosters upside down, and only allowed them to hold roosters in their arms, because he was born in the year of rooster. This shows the emperor's special favor for his sign of the zodiac.

There are some stories showing a relationship between the rooster and the zodiac. Wang Anshi, a famous politician of the Song Dynasty, was born in the year of rooster. Feeling envious, one of his political opponents asked someone to paint a picture in which a man was shooting down a rooster with an arrow. He told others that the shooter was himself, and that the rooster he had shot was Wang Anshi. The painting implied that, he had ousted Wang Anshi from an official position. Soon after that, he submitted a written statement to a higher authority accusing Wang Anshi of mismanagement. Not only was his plan frustrated, but he himself was degraded. Then he told others, "The rooster which had been shot down was none other than myself."

There are many strange roosters described in the fairy tales. As recorded in a book, there was a rooster that originated in Korea that had a tail almost two meters long. According to *On the Supplement of Omissions*, the State of Yuezhi in the Western Regions once offered a double-headed and four-footed rooster as a tribute. When one of its heads crowed, the other would also follow. *The Brief History of the State of Wei* recorded a four-footed and four-winged rooster, which was regarded as s dragon. Anyone who killed it would die. Rooster of odd shapes were often regarded as ominous animals. For example, if a black rooster has a white head, people who ate it would become ill. Roosters with six feet, four feet, or five colors were regarded as man-killers.

However, some strange roosters were quite interesting. As recorded in the *Stories of Ghosts and Men*, a man named Song Chuzong bought a rooster that often crowed, and he was fond of it. He put it in a cage by the window, and the resourceful rooster began to talk like a man. By talking with the rooster every day, Song Chuzong became quite skilled in debate.

Finally, we will mention an idiom, "rise up upon hearing the crow of a rooster and practice with a sword." This idiom derives from a general named Zu Di of the Eastern Jin Dynasty who resolved to recover the land that had been invaded and occupied by alien people. Every day he would rise to read books on the art of war or to brandish spears and sticks upon hearing the crow of a rooster. Therefore, the idiom is used to describe people with a firm resolve to succeed.

11. Dog

The dog had an old alias, Panhu, and legends about it can be traced to times of great antiquity.

It is said that Gao Xin, head of a tribe, had a dog named Panhu. At that time, there was a war in China among the tribes. Among them the Quanrong tribe had strong soldiers. Gao Xin could not defeat them. He therefore put up a notice that he would marry his daughter to anyone who could capture the leader of the enemy troops. His dog, Panhu, rushed into the enemy position, and caught the ringleader. Gao Xin, awarded his daughter to the dog as promised. Panhu brought the girl to the Nanshan Mountain where they married and gave birth to six boys and six girls; the boys and girls later married among themselves, and carried on the family line for generations. They eventually became a clan called Nanman in the ancient times. Even today, some of the southern ethnic minorities regard Panhu as their ancestor, and various legends about this are circulated among them.

The *Stories of Immortals* also recorded stories about Panhu. During the reign of Gao Xin, an old woman in the palace had an ear disease and picked a worm from her ear. She put it in a bottle gourd (*hu*), and covered it with a plate (*pan*). Soon afterwards the worm changed into a dog of various colors. The dog has been called Panhu since then, and the bottle gourd became the idol of clans in remote antiquity. The legend that Nü Wa and Fu Xi rode on a bottle gourd to save themselves from a flood was circulated among the She, Yao, Miao, Dong and other ethnic groups in the southwest China. They bore sons and daughters and became the earliest ancestors of human beings. Researchers believe that this story reflects the life of clans that lived by collecting plants, and had the bottle gourd as their totem. As society progressed, humans developed to the stage where they could train dogs, and the totem changed from a bottle gourd into a dog. According to historical records, there was a portrait of the deceased Panhu on Wushan Mountain in the western Hunan, which was that of a dog. Moreover, some of the southern ethnic groups have kept to the present day the custom of not allowing people to curse, kill, or eat dogs.

Among the various tamed animals, the dog is man's most faithful companion. As mentioned before, a horse is faithful to its owner, but not everyone has the means by which to keep a horse, while dog-raising is possible for anyone and most of the dogs are loyal and devoted to their owners. There are many stories about the friendship between a man and his dog. According to the *Stories of Immortals*, a man named Yang Sheng raised a dog and the dog always stayed with him. Once, Yang Sheng was dead drunk on the grassland when a fire broke out. It was winter, the wind was strong, and the fire was burning fiercely. The dog cried loudly, but could not wake up Yang Sheng, It ran away to get wet and returned to shake itself and spray water around its owner. After the fire went out, the grass around Yang Sheng was not burned because it had been wetted, and so the man's life was saved. On another occasion, Yang Sheng fell into a dry well because of carelessness when walking at night. The dog wailed beside the mouth of the well. At daybreak someone happened to pass by and saw the dog crying there. Being curious, the man walked over and found Yang Sheng in the well. Yang Sheng promised that if the man pulled him out, he would be richly rewarded. The man asked for the dog as his reward. Yang Sheng said that by barking it had saved his life, and so he could give the man anything except the dog. The man therefore refused to pull Yang Sheng out of the well. At that moment, the dog popped its head into the well. Yang Sheng understood the meaning of this, and agreed to give the dog to the man. So the man helped Yang Sheng get out, and left with the dog. Five days later, the dog returned home.

Though there were exaggerations in such stories about dogs saving their owners from calamity, such things might really happen. However, this story about a dog named Huang Er delivering letters is more like a fairy tale. Lu Ji, a man of great learning during the Western Jin Dynasty, loved to hunt when he was young. One of his friends gave him a dog named Huang Er. Later, Lu Ji brought that dog with him when he moved from a region south of the Yangtze River to Luoyang where he had been appointed to a government post. The dog was so intelligent it could understand human language. Lu Ji stayed at Luoyang for a long time without hearing from his family. He said jokingly to the dog, "I have not received any letter from my family for a long time. Could you convey a message for me?" The dog wagged its tail and barked happily as if showing agreement. Thinking that there would be no harm in giving it a try, Lu Ji tied a bamboo tube containing a letter to the dog's neck, and the dog then started off. Lu Ji's family lived in Wudi, and there were many rivers on the way. The dog would signal by wagging its tail whenever it came to a river. Seeing the lovely animal, people who happened to be crossing the river would take it across with them. At last, the dog reached its destination. It held the bamboo tube in its mouth, and gave out noises as soon as it saw Lu Ji's family. They opened the tube and read the letter. The dog then barked as if expecting something. The family put their reply in the bamboo tube and tied it on the dog's neck. It then started its return journey. Soon afterward it arrived at Lu Ji's home. The dog took half a month to make the round trip, while a man would have to spend more than a month to cover the same distance. When the dog died, Lu Ji took it back to his hometown, and buried it ceremoniously. The villagers called its tomb the grave of Huang Er.

Because dogs have helped people in various ways, many of their deeds of loyalty to their owners or helping others have been recorded in history and fairy tales. However, though a dog may sacrifice its life to save its owner, it may not be so friendly towards others. Sometimes a dog even looks quite ferocious. One fable says that there was a wineshop selling good wine at a reasonable price, yet nobody came to drink. The wine went bad because it was kept too long. The owner was puzzled. Others told him, "Your wine is really good, but the dog at your gate looks so terrible, baring its fangs and brandishing its claws. People was frightened. Who would dare to enter the house for a drink?" This story was originally told to monarchs, to show them that although they might be excellent, if there were bad elements among their subordinates, others would not dare to go to them for shelter. However, we can see another side to a dog's habits and characteristics from this story. It is true that a dog will sometimes do evil deeds on the strength of its master's power, hence the Chinese idiom "to behave like a dog relying upon the power of its master's"; moreover, a dog might also do bad things for its master, hence the Chinese word "lackey."

Thus dogs were not always righteous in the fairy tales. Some of them were harmful to people, and others were even dog ghosts. According to the *Stories of Immortals*, there was a pavilion at the foot of Lushan Mountain. Anyone who passed there at night would became ill or die. It is said that it was often haunted by over ten black-and-white men and women. Once a man named Zhi Boyi put up for the night there. He was still reading at the midnight when some of these people suddenly appeared, sitting beside him and amusing themselves by gambling. Looking at them in the mirror, he discovered that they were actually dogs. So he burned one man's clothes intentionally and found that it gave out the smell of burned fur. Zhi Boyi caught another of these dogs and stabbed it. At first it cried like a man, but then it became a dead dog.

The ancient books also recorded some strange dogs. For example, according to *The Classic of Mountains and Rivers*, there was a blue dog that ate people starting from the head and working downwards. There was also a heavenly dog that looked like a fox with a white head. It lived on Yinshan Mountain. Another book says that there was a white dog during the seventh year of the Tai Kang period of the Jin Dynasty with a height of one meter. Its whole body shone with light and it always crouched when nobody was around and left whenever it saw people.

12. Pig

Among the twelve animals of the zodiac, the pig is last, probably because it looks ugly and leads a coarse life. The pig's appearance—two nostrils towards the sky and a fat body—can't escape people's ridicule. Moreover, its diet is so coarse that it can eat almost anything. It is impossible for people not to look down upon it. Even the pig itself feels ashamed of its ungainly appearance. As recorded in a book, someone offered a large pig to King Zhao of Yan as a tribute. After it was killed, the pig appeared in the Prime Minister's dream, and said, "Heaven made me ugly and eat the dirtiest things. Now, thanks to your help, I have become a river god in the nether world." It seems that the pig was transformed after being killed.

It was humble while alive, and became noble after death. People thought highly of pork, especially in ancient times when few could afford to eat it. Only those who had high positions could eat pork. It was a delicious food and was often offered as a valuable and treasured gift.

The pig was also depicted as an intelligent animal in fairy tales and legends. A tale says that there were four brothers who made a living by killing pigs. One day a pig which was about to be killed suddenly cried out loudly for help. Thinking that the brothers were fighting, the neighbors ran over and found that it was the pig which was talking. The brothers were deeply moved and stopped killing pigs after that. All of them were converted to Buddhism. Buddhists often used this story to advocate the monastic discipline of not killing livestock. There were also stories about pigs preaching and being reincarnated as spirits. As recorded in *A Grove of Pearl in the Dharma Garden*, there was a rich man named Du Yuan during the Jin Dynasty. His son, Tian Bao, who liked chanting Buddhist scriptures, died of a sudden illness at the age of ten. Five months after his death, an old female pig gave birth to five piglets, and one of them was quite fat. Soon after that Du's superior came. Du Yuan wanted to entertain the man with the fattest piglet, and ordered people to kill it. Suddenly a monk appeared, telling him that the piglet was none other than his deceased son. Then the monk disappeared. At that moment, the piglet rose into the air and clouds filled the sky for a long time. Obviously, because the child had chanted scriptures, he had become a Buddha after his death.

Some stories about pigs have moral significance. As recorded in *Han Ying's Illustrations of the Didactic Application of the Classic of Songs*, when Mencius was a little boy he saw his neighbor killing pigs and so he asked his mother why they did it. His mother jokingly told him that they were killing pigs to give him some pork. However, she felt regretful as soon as she said this, thinking to herself, "When I was conceiving the child, I would not sit on a mat if it was not placed correctly, and I would not eat meat if it was not rightly cut. When I was pregnant I tried to do everything right. Now the child is growing up, if I lie to him, he will not keep faith later. That will never do." So she bought pork from the neighbor for the child. This is one of the many stories about "Mencius' mother teaching her son." It reveals that only if adults set the right example can their children follow the correct path.

The *Supplementary Biography of Dong Zheng* described the easy manner of Sima Hui, a famous man during the Three Kingdoms Period. Once his neighbor lost a pig, and thought Sima Hui's pig might be his. Without any argument, Sima Hui let the man lead the pig away. Several days later, the neighbor found his lost pig, and came to Sima Hui's house to return the pig and apologize. Instead of blaming him, Sima Hui expressed his gratitude. He was really a modest and self-disciplined man, who had great wisdom but sometimes behaved like a fool.

There are some famous men and scholars who did not regard the task of herding pigs as a disgrace. For example, Wu You's father, a high-ranking official, died when he was twenty. Wu You, however, refused to receive aid from the court. He made his living by herding pigs, while chanting scriptures. Once a friend of his father said, "You were the son of a high-ranking official, yet you make your living by herding pigs. Even if you don't care if you lose face, you should consider your deceased father!" Wu You simply went off laughing, and still herded pigs while reading scriptures. Another story is about Liang Hong. Though he was poor, he had a strong and upright character. He was a great scholar, yet made his living by herding pigs. Such stories show people's exemplary conduct and nobility by their doing such low and degrading work as herding pigs.

Another story tells that Zhang Heng, a writer during the Han Dynasty, had extraordinary painting skills. Once he saw a magic pig, which looked rather ugly. It had a pig's body and man's head. Even ghosts disliked it. The pig often appeared standing on a rock by the river. It escaped into the water when it found Zhang Heng trying to paint a picture of it. Later Zhang Heng did not move his hands when he saw the pig, but secretly drew a picture of it with his toes in the sand on the ground. The painting was a good likeness of the animal.

Though the pig looks ugly, many people born in the year of pig did not detest and reject it; some powerful people even enshrined and worshipped it as a god. An emperor, named Zhu Houzhao in the Ming Dynasty, was born in the Year of Pig, and his family name was Zhu (a homonym for "pig"—*zhu* in Chinese), he was unwilling to see people be disrespectful toward pigs. So he issued an order forbidding people throughout China to kill pigs in the Year of Pig. This can be regarded as giving special care to pigs.

In conclusion, we will mention the Pig Zhu Bajie in the classic novel *Journey to the West*, who is the most famous and favorite pig figure in literary history. He always addressed himself as "Lao Zhu," which makes people laugh. There are many interesting stories about this pig. Readers who are interested in him might well read *Journey to the West*.

III. The Zodiac Animals and Folk Customs

The worship of the zodiac animals is found in various folk customs, and here we will introduce some of these customs that are directly related to each animal. The folk customs are generally seen in the countryside. From them we can learn about the hopes and feelings that people have placed in the animals and something of their own eternal charm.

1. Mouse

The Han people have a tradition of celebrating Mouse Day, which is on the 25th day of the first month of the lunar year. On this day people in the south of Zhejiang Province like to play a game called Destroying Mice's Eyes, which is said to be efficacious in eliminating mice. The people stand at the west end of the room and throw boiled black soy beans over the root beams towards the east end, mumbling as they do so, "Up at the western end, down at the eastern end, giving the mice a quick end." It is believed that only the beans which go over the beams and fall at the eastern end count toward removing the mice.

Smoking out the mouse is a folk custom of the Koreans in Northeast China. On the first day of the first month of the lunar year, children put straw on the ground and burn it, and the peasants calculate their coming harvest according to the size of the fire. As a matter of fact, this activity does smoke out and kill some of the pests, including the mouse, and it reinforces soil fertility.

In some compact Han communities in Qinghai Province, people will steam twelve "blind" dough mice, whose eyes are made of pepper seeds, on the fourteenth day of the first month of the lunar year. Early the next day, which is the traditional Lantern Festival, the people will put these dough mice on an altar and bow to them, begging the mice to eat weeds instead of crops so as to ensure a bumper harvest.

In the past, people of Shanghai had a special method to resolve the problem of "mice droppings," as they thought the droppings of a food-searching mouse were an evil omen of disaster and illness. They went to the countryside to ask many households for rice, and then returned home to cook the "rice from one hundred households." It was believed that when this rice was eaten, disasters and illness would disappear.

People on Chongming Islet, near Shanghai, often imagined that the squeaks of mice was the sound of them counting coins, and took this to be an evil omen. In order to ward off calamity, the people would be especially careful in their daily lives, and some of them were likely to go to the temple to burn incense and pray for good luck. Only when nothing serious occurred after several days did they set their minds at rest.

Some people living in Shanghai area thought that a mouse gnawing at clothes during the night was a punishment for their having said evil things about them. In light of this, people avoided talking about mice or doing harm to mice when they heard such gnawing.

In the history of Chinese folk customs, the most popular one relating to the mouse is "the mouse marrying off its daughter," and a special day was selected to celebrate the mouse daughter's wedding. This is on the night of the 25th day of the first month of the lunar year. When that time comes, people usually turn off all their lights and sit quietly at bed, eating dough mouse paws, scorpion tails, and fried soy beans in darkness. They sit quietly in darkness to avoid any disturbance to the mouse's wedding, and eat the "mouse paws" to hurry up the process and the "scorpion tails" to protect mice from scorpions.

In the Jianghan Plain area of Hubei Province, people usually don't husk rice or grin wheat and children should keep quiet on the Mouse Daughter's Wedding Day, because people there think mice will make noise all the year around if they are disturbed on this day.

The Hans in different areas have selected different days for the mouse to take a wife. In the north of Jiangsu Province, this occurs on the 16th day of the first month of the lunar year, while in the south, it is on the first day of the first month. In Hunan Province, it is on the fourth day of the second month of the lunar year, and in Sichuan Province, it's on New Year's Eve. In the southern area of the Yangtze River, people usually make sesame candies and popcorn on the mouse's wedding day. When night comes, children put these foods in places often haunted by mice and beat iron pot covers and dustpans loudly to give a warm welcome to the mouse's bride.

The custom of celebrating the mouse's wedding is a tribute of the exuberant vitality and fertility of mice. People often draw pictures and make paper-cuts about the wedding according to their imaginations, and paste these on the wall of a bridal chamber so as to wish for a rapidly growing family.

2. Ox

It is said that the fifth day of the first lunar month is the day of the ox, in memory of its birthday. People predict good or bad fortunes of their ox raising by the weather of this day: a fine day indicates prosperity, a cloudy day indicates disaster. Also on this day people treat the ox with much care; hitting it and killing it are forbidden. In some places people even feed the ox rice. Many people burn incense, worship gods in the Ox King Temples, and watch operas. They thus entertain themselves by celebrating the birthday of the ox.

Chinese ethnic groups also have the custom that salute the ox. The Buyi ethnic group in Lizhi, Luodian, Anlong, and Ceting in Guizhou Province celebrate the birthday of the ox on the eighth day of the fourth lunar month. They let the oxen rest and feed them fine polished glutinous rice. People of the Gelo ethnic group who live in Zunyi, Renhuai, and Zhenning in Guizhou Province, celebrate their festival of the king of oxen (also called festival of the ox-god) on the first day of the tenth lunar month. On this day, they don't let an ox work and put two glutinous rice cakes made of fine polished glutinous rice on its horns, and then lead it by the water so that it can see its shadow in the water. In this way, people want the ox to be happy on its birthday. The Zhuang people has the same custom. On this day, people are not permitted to beat, blame and ride an ox or have the ox work in the fields. They tie the ox to the door and put a table there with steamed glutinous rice, toasted cakes and flowers on it. They burn incense and make a slight bow with their hands folded and say to the animal, "The king of oxen, you worked hard during the past year and provided food for us. Now, please try some glutinous rice and cakes for your labor."

The people of the Zhuang ethnic group who live in Jingxi, Napo, Debao, and Daxin, have a traditional ox spirit festival. This takes place at different times in different places, but generally on the eighth day of the fourth lunar month, though sometimes on the seventh day of the fifth lunar month, the sixth day of the sixth lunar month, or the seventh day of the seventh lunar month. On this day, people let the ox rest while they clean the cattle pen. Girls lead the ox to the water and wash them with mugwort leaves and a little sweet rice wine to eliminate lice and calm their souls. In some places, people let the children lead the ox to hills in the early morning so that it can enjoy the festival freely. They put chicken or duck, and steamed five-color glutinous rice together with sweet wine, chicken soup or mung bean soup into a thick bamboo tube to feed the ox as thanks for their labor. When feeding the ox, children wrap red paper around the ox horns and the whole family congratulates the ox on its birthday.

The Dong people, who live in Rongjiang and Dongjiang of Guizhou Province, have a traditional washing ox festival on the sixth day of the sixth lunar month. When spring ploughing is finished, they lead the oxen to the river and wash them. At the same time they put some feathers from a killed chicken or duck on the cattle pens to welcome the oxen, and pray for peace and robustness for the oxen.

The above-mentioned festivals for the ox were popular in southwestern ethnic groups in China. Such specific festivals for the ox are not only because oxen play an important role in people's lives and work but also relate to the history and traditions of the different ethnic groups. Take the Gelo ethnic group as an example. It is said that long, long ago, the Gelo people lived a hard life in a high land with many rocks and less water. In order to find a better place to live, they started on an expedition with their only ox. When their food ran out, the ox disappeared. After it came back, crystal clear white rice fell from the sky like a stream of water. Later, the ox took the people to a cultivated and beautiful place where the Gelo people settled and lived a happy life. The people of Gelo set the first day of the tenth lunar month as the ox's birthday and established the Counting on Ox Festival to thank the ox for its help. Another legend is about an ox-skin drums spread among the Miao people. It is said that there was a volume of classics given by a god to every tribe, in which the name of their ancestors and their origins and migrations were recorded. In order to let one's soul go back home, these classics had to be read when a person died. However, the classics were eaten by a supernatural ox, and changed into the skin of an ox's belly. The ox told the people that they should make the ox belly into a drum. Then, when a person died, his soul could go back home when the drum was beaten. All these kinds of legends about oxen have made the ox god in people's minds, hence the festivals for the ox.

The significance of the ox is reflected not only in the birthday and festivals of the king of oxen, but also in folk customs such as the ceremony offering sacrifices to gods or ancestors, weddings and funerals, and many features of daily life.

China, in early times, had the custom of praying for rain by killing an ox. It is said that there was a pool in which lay a stone ox in ancient times. Whenever there was drought, people would kill a live ox and put the blood and mud on the back of this stone ox, and then they would pray. It would rain after they finished praying. The sky would become clear until the mud was cleaned off the stone ox by the rain. People also had the custom of sacrificing an ox in spring time. They made wooden images of the spring ox and a spring god to a size in accordance with the twelve-month period of time, 365 days and 24 solar terms, so as to comply with climate to guarantee good weather for the crops.

There is kind of funeral called "jumping yak" in the area where the Naxi ethnic group lives. After an old person dies, his ashes are put into a cloth bag. At the funeral, all his relatives participate. His family members burn a fire in the yard, and people dance together in a circle, the leading person singing a funeral song. When the dance and song are finished, the people bow before the bag of ashes one after another. Then, a yak is brought forward and the people pour a cup of milk tea into its ear. If it jumps, that is a good sign; if not, they change the yak for another one. After that the yak is killed by the robust young men whose parents still alive. Generally, the heart of the yak is taken first, then the skin and the meat. The heart and meat are placed before the bag of ashes. This is called the raw sacrifice.

Then, people cook the meat and offer it again, a ceremony known as the ripe sacrifice. After all these things are done, the bag of ashes is buried.

The ox also appears in the marital customs of many ethnic groups. A "snatch the ox tail" custom is popular within the Miao ethnic group in the northwest of Guizhou Province. After an engagement, the bride's side must raise an ox. At the wedding, the ox is brought in with two of its legs fastened. Both the bride and bridegroom are accompanied by more than ten young people. The bride must first cut off the ox tail, and then flee from the bridegroom who chases the tail, while the guards on bride's side protect her. According to this custom, the bridegroom must capture the tail before the bride's parents arrive or they cannot get married. No doubt, if the bride loves her bridegroom, she will not make things too difficult for him.

The She ethnic group in Zhejiang Province has the custom of the "trail-blazing ox" in their wedding ceremonies. The bride's family must select a strong calf and drape it with bands of colorful silk. As the bride gets into her sedan, the bridegroom walks ahead with the ox to blaze trail so as to prevent disaster and to pray for peace and luck. There is another saying about this "trail-blazing ox" custom. It is said that it is not auspicious for two women to get married together and walk the same road. After negotiations, the one with the longest distance to go first. Then the bridegroom of the other side takes an ox with red cloth tied to its horns, this ox is called the "trail-blazing ox." As the bridegroom walks with this ox, the road thus "blazed" becomes new and so cannot harm the wedding.

The ox is also sometimes used as a birthday present, but in name only. In the Liuba Area of Shaanxi Province, the celebration of an elder's birthday is called "go to the ox king fair." Because the ox works hard and is helpful to humans, people show their respect for elders in the name of the ox. "Go to the ox king fair" is a party to celebrate the elder's birthday. People bring presents, while the elder provides a rich banquet for the guests and urges people, one by one, to drink. After the dinner, people engage in many entertainments throughout the night until the next day.

Many folk entertainments are related to the ox. A kind of "ox story" is popular in Hancheng where Han people live in Shaanxi Province. Whenever the festival is held, several trained oxen are selected and several children who are good at driving oxen dress up as historical figures. Each child stands on the back of an ox. To the accompaniment of a rhythmical drum, the oxen move slowly and the children take different postures, vivid and interesting.

An "ox lamp" performance is popular in the areas where Han people live in Sichuan Province. The show is usually performed during the Spring Festival. Its name comes from the ox-shaped dancing masks that are used and the singing of a "lamp song."

The Miao, Dong and Li ethnic groups all have the sports activity known as a "bullfight." Usually held at festivals, two oxen fight each other in such bullfights. Different ethnic groups have different ceremonies and rules. Take Dong for an example. The first step in their traditional bullfight ceremony is to send the letter of challenge. This is followed by the second step, the entry ceremony, in which honor guards walk to the place where the bullfight is to be held, led by a man holding a sign that announces their presence. This front man is followed by a gong and drum team and the ox. Behind them come a team of people with different flags. The third step is bullfight itself. The "ox head man" (host) for each side holds fire sticks while two persons lead two oxen together. At the sound of a gun, each ox head man throws away his fire sticks and the persons leading the oxen leave. Then the two oxen rush to fight each other. The losing ox will later be killed and its meat shared by both sides. The ox that wins can enjoy red rice and sweet wine. When the bullfight ends, the girls of victorious side come forward to snatch the flags and ox saddles from the losing side and hang them on their own drum tower.

Finally, we'd like to introduce a food made of ox meat, called "lamp shadow beef." Originally produced in Sichuan Province, the most famous lamp shadow beef comes from Daxian County. It has this name because it is a thin and diaphanous slice of dried beef that somewhat resembles the material from which the characters in a Chinese shadow play are made (painted animal skins). Lamp shadow beef is red, hot and sweet.

3. Tiger

Some Chinese ethnic groups worship a white tiger as the mountain god. The Hezhen ethnic group offers sacrifices to the tiger on every third day of the third lunar month and every ninth day of the ninth lunar month.

The Tujia ethnic group considers the white tiger to be a god which is divided into a charitable "resident white tiger" and an evil "roaming white tiger." The people offer sacrifices to the resident white tiger, while the roaming white tiger is shunned. The roaming white tiger is often considered to be the cause of infantile convulsions in children, so people ask a wizard to "wipe away the white tiger." They put a chair outside the door to which a white cock is fastened, while the wizard exercises magic inside the house. If the cock crows, this means the white tiger has gone.

In the Shanxi, Hebei and Henan areas, people sometimes call a stone mill the white tiger god. During the Spring Festival, they paste paper with the words "very lucky the white tiger" onto the stone mill so they will have peace.

There is a custom of "touching the steamed tiger-shaped bun" in Huaxian County, Shaanxi Province. Before a wedding, the bridegroom's uncle is expected to steam a pair of tiger-shaped buns tied together by a red string. As soon as the bride arrives, the buns are put around her neck. After she enters the room, the buns are take off and shared by the bride and bridegroom, which indicates happiness. Each bun is different. One is male, with the character for "king" on its head. This means that the husband is the lord of the family. The other tiger is female, with a pair of birds on its head. This signifies that the wife will follow her husband. A little tiger inscribed on each tiger's neck signifies hope that the couple will have a child early.

On Chongming Island near Shanghai, the bride has the custom of wearing tiger-headed shoes. When the bride wears a pair of tiger-headed shoes, it means that the woman can bring her husband under control with the strength of a tiger. And in some northwest areas, the bride's dowry includes a flour tiger, a tiger-headed hat, a tiger-headed pillow, etc., which are thought to prevent evil.

In ancient China, it was a custom to wash an infants' body with liquid tiger-bone extract. It was said that the child would keep healthy all its lifetime if this was done. Another custom for children is to wear tiger-headed shoes. Made of yellow cloth, the tiger-headed shoes are embroidered with a tiger head that has the character "king" in the middle of its forehead. When the child has his first birthday or other birthdays, his parents will let him wear tiger-headed shoes to prevent evil and build up his courage. In Xifu of Shaanxi Province, people send a cloth tiger to baby boy when he is one month old. The sender will be his uncle. This means that the family hopes the boy will grow to be as strong as a tiger. In some places in Shanxi Province, there is a custom of sending children tiger-shaped pillows. The tiger-shaped pillows will be given by the uncle on a child's birthday as a blessing.

In some places, people paint tigers on cocoons, paper or mugwort leaves as decorations to wear during the Dragon Boat Festival. This is thought to prevent evil.

The Gelo ethnic group, which lives in Guangxi, used to celebrate the first tiger's day before the 15th day of the eighth lunar month. That day, the whole village would kill a bull and take out its heart to divide between the families so that each may have a portion to use for a sacrifice to their ancestors. The leftover beef was used by the villagers for a dinner party.

4. Rabbit

In many places, people have the custom of "hanging a rabbit's head." On the first day of the first lunar month, people hang a rabbit's head made of flour on the front of their doors to prevent evil and disaster.

The rabbit is auspicious and has a reputation for longevity so that the custom of "putting a rabbit into the arms" is in vogue among fishermen of the Shandong coastal areas. During every Grain Rain period (one of the 24 solar periods that begins on April 19, 20, or 21 and is the right time for sowing in North China) and Pure Brightness period (one of the 24 solar periods that begins on April 4, 5, or 6 and is the time for people to sweep graves), as soon as the husband returns, the wife will unexpectedly put a white rabbit into her husband's arms in the hope of preserving his happiness and peace at sea.

In some places, people have the practice of sending hare pictures to children. Such pictures depict a person standing on a table holding a hare, surrounded by six children. These pictures are a way to bless children so that they may steadily rise in their careers and have happy life.

In many places, rabbit meat is not to be eaten by pregnant women because this may cause a child to be born with a harelip.

5. Dragon

In North China people believe it's good luck to see a "dangling dragon," for legend has it that wherever a dragon goes, clouds move around it. On windy days, as clouds are rolling by one may see vertical thing in the clouds. People think that they are dangling dragons. As a custom, people offer sacrifices to dragon god in dragon temples, especially during drought days. According to some folk beliefs, the thirteenth day of the fifth lunar month is the birthday of the dragon, and on this day it should rain. So there is a saying: "After the thirteenth of the fifth lunar month there will be no drought."

In some places of Guangdong people enshrine the Dragon Mother and offer sacrifices to her on the eighth day of the fifth lunar month each year. It is said that the Dragon Mother was an aged widow named Wen Ao who made her living by weaving. One day as she was gathering vegetables in the field, she found five eggs. She put these into her basket and went back home. A few days later, five baby-dragons came out of the eggs. Wen Ao brought them to a river and released them into the water. Then one day when she passed by the river, the dragons came out of the water and played around her. The local people heard of this and enshrined her as the Dragon Mother and a temple was built to her memory where sacrifices are offered.

Each year, every Chinese ethnic group holds special offering ceremonies for the dragon related to their particular ethnic group. The Bai people take the second day of the second lunar month as the birthday of their Ancestral Dragon. On this day each family burns incense and makes sacrifices to the Ancestral Dragon, offering steamed bread in the shape of a dragon, tiger, monkey or phoenix. They also hold an activity of "dragon-seeding." That refers to the seeding of watermelon because the weaving of the trailing branches of watermelon vines look like a dragon. People on this day have their hair cut and washed, symbolizing the "dragon raising its head." All these activities will be led by a man born in the year of the dragon, and a family may ask a relative for help in this matter if no family member is born in such a year. Some other activities are also held by communities such as the performance of dragon dance. An elderly man born in the year of dragon takes the lead holding a dragon and twelve women, also born in the year of dragon, perform the dragon dance with him. A crowd of people follow, singing and dancing. The most interesting activity is called "lazy-dragon-catching." Twelve men wearing animal skins and masks take the roles of the twelve animal zodiac gods, and the dragon man plays the part of a lazy dragon. Surrounded by the "twelve gods," the lazy dragon has to jump and leap all the time while the "gods" try to catch him with rattan rings. When he is finally caught, he has to repent before the public for his laziness.

On the third day of the third lunar month, the Bai people hold a ceremony called "dragon-inviting." Twelve men born in the year of dragon go towards a spring performing a dragon dance with a straw dragon as they progress. Then they drench the straw dragon with water from the spring and, throw fruit, items made of flour and other offerings into the spring. After that they bring the spring water back to the village. At the end of ceremony, they put the straw dragon at the entrance to their village and spread the spring water onto the watermelon fields—symbolizing the sowing of "seeds of dragon." So they think they will have enough water to irrigate their fields and will have a good harvest.

A ploughing ceremony is held on the day that summer begins (one of the 24 solar terms, around the May 5, 6 or 7). People wrap vine branches around their ploughs to give them the shape of the Big Dipper, symbolizing the Ancestral Dragon. After this, they begin to plough. All earthworms that are uncovered by the ploughing are protected and released into water, called "sending the dragon back to its palace." So they will have good weather for crops.

The Bai people hold an ash spreading ceremony during the fifth lunar month. Each family burns the rubbish gathered from inside and outside their courtyards and then spreads the ash on their fields. They call this "protecting the seeds of the dragon."

It is also said that the dragon comes down to inspect the human world on the twenty-fourth day of the sixth lunar month. To light the surroundings and guide its way, people hang lanterns, decorated with nine dragons and fortune stars, on the trees at the entrance to their village, and put floating lanterns on the water surface.

The twenty-fourth day of the seventh lunar month is named the Water-thanking day. On this day people put watermelon vines and leaves on the surface of the water, and present various offerings so that the dragon will stay at home and the weather will remain sunny during the coming harvest days. On the eighth day of the eighth lunar month people start to gather in the crops. On this day a man born in the dragon year will be the first to cut the crops with his sickle.

The Bai people believe that on the tenth day of the tenth lunar month the dragon settles down for winter, and so ceremonies are held on that day. In the eleventh lunar month, people go to the mountains to hunt after giving an offering to the dragon. From the first to the fifteenth day of the first lunar month various activities are held in memory of the Ancestral Dragon.

From the above-listed customs we can see that the Bai people relate their lives to the dragon all the year long. Some other Chinese ethnic groups also have their own customs related to dragon. The Han Chinese take the second day of the second lunar month as the dragon's day. In north China, each housewife knocks on the brim of a pot with a stick on the morning of that day, a practice called "shaking the worms." They also make clusters with thin sorghum stalks and colored paper and hang these on the roof beams in imitation of a dragon with its head up and its tail dropping down. On this day, the fried wheat cakes are called "dragon scale cakes," the noodles "dragon whiskers noodles," and the vegetable balls "dragon eggs." Women stop sewing on this day so as to avoid hurting the eyes of the dragon with their needles. In South China, the twentieth day of the fifth lunar month is titled the "separating day for dragons." People say that on this day, dragons living in heaven leave their parents for the districts under their control. Feeling sad, the young dragons cannot help making tears. That is why there is a lot of rain in the fifth lunar month south of the Yangtze River. People in the southern part of Anhui Province hold a "welcoming candle dragon" ceremony to pray for the birth of a son. In a couple of days around the fifteenth of the first lunar month a special dragon dance team will come to the towns and villages, and those married women who have given birth only to girls will wait for the dragon at the entrance to their villages, each with a red candle in her hands. When the dragon team arrives, they ask the dancers to exchange their candle for a candle on the dragon's head. Then the women take this and put it in their bedrooms which would ensure that they will bear a boy next. If they do give birth to a son that year, they will reward the dragon with gifts.

These dragon memorial ceremonies usually include entertainment. The most popular one is the dragon dance. Dragon dances vary a great deal according to the shape of dragon and the manner of dancing. There are the fire-dragon dance, yarn-dragon dance, straw-dragon dance, black-dragon dance, rolling-dragon dance and drunk-dragon dance. Especially popular in Shanxi Province, the dragon dance was given particular care by people in the old days. During a drought season in spring, people might dance the big gray dragon, in which a big dragon was surrounded by seven smaller ones, heading toward the East, and the distance between them is three meters. The dragon dancers abstained from eating meat for three days before they dressed themselves in their dark gray suits for the dance. During the show, the dance was accompanied by gongs, drums and five crackers, giving a very grand scene. Nowadays, dragon dances are performed not only on festival days related to the dragon, but also in many other local festivals and celebrations.

In South China, especially in Hunan and Hubei provinces, dragon boat racing is a common local sport. In memory of Qu Yuan (340-278 B.C.), the first great Chinese poet, the boat races are held during the Dragon Boat Festival day (the fifth day of the fifth lunar month). It is said that the local people tried to rescue Qu Yuan in their dragon boat after he plunged into the river and drowned. The boat itself is a dragon-shaped wooden boat, with a raised dragon head at the ship's bow. Each dragon boat is driven by more than ten peddlers and a drummer to keep them rowing in rhythm. When the race begins, the drummer begins to beat his drum and the peddlers begin to row with their oars. The audience gathered all along both banks enjoys the race greatly. The whole scene can be quite exciting.

Chinese food also has some relation to the dragon. Dragon whiskers noodles, for instance, can be as thin as the dragon whiskers. They are made by continuous pulling and drawing of the dough. To make this is truly a unique skill. Dragon and Phoenix Cakes are a special local food made for marriage ceremonies in Yunnan Province. The family of bridegroom makes these cakes as a gift in return for receiving the dowry. The cakes, made of flour, are engraved with the picture of a dragon and phoenix, as a blessing on the couples "for their prosperous and happy life."

6. Snake

Many snake king temples were built in some places in ancient China. The Snake King Temple in Suzhou City, with a statue of the General Snake in it, is one of these. As the legend goes, the twelfth day of the fourth lunar month is the birthday of the Snake King. A great many people go to the Snake King Temple to pray on that day. The people believe that to attach a *fulu* (lines or pictures drawn by the priest to protect people from harm by ghosts and other evils, or to bring luck) to windows may keep snakes away. It is also said that the earliest pilgrims to the Snake King Temple were frog-hunters; they prayed to the Snake King for mercy, for they made their living by taking the food from the mouths of snakes.

Snake worship can still be seen in many places south of the Yangtze River. People there differentiate between domestic snakes and wild ones. Domestic snakes, they believe, may bring them good fortune, as they are said to take rice from the rich and give it to the poor, and to increase supply rice to an inexhaustible amount. People believe that a mouse will scream in fear when it encounters a snake. In some places people take it as a bad luck to see a snake fall to the ground, leave its cave, or shed its skin. So the saying is: "a down-falling snake brings a male bad luck; a cave-exiting one, a female." People in Yixing, Jiangsu Province, give a special offering to their domestic snakes each year on the fifteenth day of the first lunar month; on the second day of the second lunar month; on the Pure Brightness day, the seventeenth day of the seventh lunar month; and during the Mid-autumn Festival, the Double Ninth Festival, and the Winter Solstice. A rice-powder snake is made and surrounded by small rice powder balls to symbolize snake eggs. Besides, it is also said that the Buddha statue in the temple of Yixing takes the shape of snake, with its body curling and head rising up.

Snake worship is also common in the south of Fujian Province. There snakes found in fields can be killed freely, but snakes found in the home should not be harmed. Aged persons are asked to drive them out of the house, for they are considered to be visitors sent by the spirits of family ancestors, and any family thus visited will enjoy harmony. People in Qinghai Province, however, believe that if anyone kills a snake in the home, other snakes will take revenge. So a snake found in a home is taken to the valley and released there.

During the Song Dynasty there was a popular custom around Kaifeng City in Henan Province called "Nailing the Flour Snake." On the first day of the first lunar month each year, people made snake figures with flour, and had three persons with different family names put an iron nail through each flour snake three times, and then bury it with cooked black beans and boiled eggs in the early morning. This, it was believed, would keep all kinds of evil away and protect a family from illness.

The fifth day of the third lunar month is the day for Waking Insects, one of the twenty-four solar terms. It is so named because from this day the weather turns warm, spring thunder is heard, and the creatures dormant in winter begin to move around. People in Guizhou believe that there will be a plague of insects if thunders is heard on this day.

People in Shanxi and Shaanxi steam a kind of cakes made of flour with a shape of curled snake. Two kernels of the sorghum are put on the top, symbolizing the eyes of the snake, and a coin is in the mouth. People make this cake to let treasures come into their houses.

7. Horse

The sixth day of the sixth lunar month is the day of the horse in Hubei, Hunan, Hebei and Zhejiang provinces. On this day, people determine their good and bad fortune for raising horses according to weather: a fine day indicates prosperity, a cloudy day indicates bad luck. People feed the horses on this day with much care and never beat or kill one so that their horses raising potential will flourish.

The Mongolian people have a traditional mare's milk festival and horse-racing festival at the end of the lunar August each year. This lasts for one day. In the early morning of that day, the herdsmen ride to the designated place dressed in their holiday best and taking with them some mare's milk. Then they kill sheep and oxen, prepare milky foods, fry fruits, burn cow-dung fire and steam hand-stewed meat. The horse race begins at sunrise. All the contestants are horses of two years age, which symbolizes the flourishing of animal husbandry and evokes people's respect for the nursing of mare's milk. After the race, a banquet begins. People toast, sing and recite poems accompanied by a stringed instrument with a scroll carved like a horse's head until night time.

The people of the Hexi Corridor in Gansu Province have the custom of "freezing a golden colt" on the eighth day of the first lunar month. Before down of that day, every family gets up and carries water home from a well or river. One bowl of water is placed in the yard to become frozen. After sunrise, the ice and a bowl of *laba* porridge (rice porridge with beans, nuts and dried fruit eaten on the eighth day of the twelfth lunar month) are buried in each family's field so as to expect a good harvest during the next year. This is called "freezing a golden colt" by the local people.

In ancient times, it was a custom all over the country to offer sacrifices to the horse. People offered sacrifices to Mazu in spring, Xianmu in summer, Mashe in autumn and Mabu in winter. Mazu was a heavenly horse and the name for a horse constellation; Xianmu was the god who first taught humans how to herd horses; Mashe was the god of the stables; Mabu was the god who brought disaster to horses. The reason for worshipping all these gods was to thank the horse for its help to people and to pray for peace for horses.

Among the Hans, there was a god known as the horse king, who was in charge of horses. It is said that the god was an official of the Western Han Dynasty called Jin Ridi. He originally was a Xiongnu man, but later surrendered to the Han Dynasty and became the official in charge of horses. His image, found in many temples of the horse king, has four arms and three eyes and has a terrible look. People offer whole sheep to the horse god on the twenty-third day of the sixth lunar month each year.

The ancient Qidan people had a white horse god. It is said that an immortal in ancient times rode this white horse eastward on the river; a heavenly maiden drove a green ox cart westward on another river. The two rivers joined at the foot of a mountain and the immortal and the heavenly maiden became husband and wife. They gave birth to eight children who multiplied and became the eight tribes of the Qidan ethnic group. Thus the Qidan people worshipped the white horse god and offered sacrifices to it each spring and autumn.

There was a marital custom called "before the horse and behind the horse" in the Qinghai area. The term pointed to the twelve zodiac animals. "Before the horse" indicated those animals that come before one's own sign, "behind the horse" was those animals that came behind. These two zodiac animals grouped respectively with other zodiac animals. The latter group was called "the malignant star before the horse," that is to say, people born in the years of these animals were to be avoided. When a bride entered a bridal chamber, her relatives who were born in the years of those animals were to be avoided. The former group was called "lucky people behind the horse," which meant that the people who were born in those years to escort the bride.

A marital custom called "drink back-horse wine" is in vogue in the Qinghai area. After the guests on the bride's side depart from the home of the bridegroom, some young people among them will return and the bridegroom's family then provides wine for them to enjoy until they leave. After a while, they may come back and drink again. This so-called "back-horse wine" can add a joyous atmosphere.

In the Hubei and Sichuan areas, there was a marital custom called "driving-cart horse." It was said that when a bride gets married, the ghosts of all generations of her family follow her and so it is possible for all kinds of demons from her side to bring pestilence to the bridegroom's side. So on the wedding day, the bridegroom's family would put a table outside the door with an incense burner on it; and ask a wizard to offer sacrifices to heaven and earth and to the god of the cart horse. At the same time they killed a chicken to prevent the ghosts from doing any harm. After a prayer, the wizard would throw a handful of rice at the bride's sedan so as to beat away the demons, and the bridegroom would salute the sedan. Then the sedan could enter the bridegroom's courtyard.

In Dengcheng of Shaanxi Province, there is a marital custom of "sending the golden horse." After the engagement, the bridegroom's side sends a horse made of gold or silver to the bride's family. If the family is not rich, they can send a horse made of yellow cloth instead. This indicates good luck and instant success.

The marital custom of "stepping on a horse stool" is popular among the Han and Manchu ethnic groups in northeast China. The horse stool is the foot stool made of wood for climbing off or onto a horse. When the bride gets out of her sedan, she steps on the stool instead of walking on the ground. In this way, evil can be avoided.

A marital custom of "proposing a marriage alliance with saber at one's back" is popular among the Miao people in Guizhou. This is a way to announce an engagement. Three times marital negotiations are needed between a loved man and woman. During the first time, the bride's side shows an unclear attitude; during the second, unclear agreement; and during the third, an agreement is reached. At this time, the bridegroom should have a saber on his back to express his formal proposal. As an auspicious thing that can overcome the evil, the saber indicates the ability to drive away beasts and resist aggression. The bride's side admits the man to the descendants of Miao people only when they see the saber. Then they happily make an engagement, or they never talk again about marriage.

The funeral custom called "burning the sedan and horse" is practiced throughout the Zhejiang area. When a person becomes critically ill, his family prepares a paper sedan and horse; then when the person is dying, the sedan and horse are burned outside the door. In this way, the dead will be able to go to the nether world by sedan and horse.

In ancient times, there was the custom of "parading around one's hometown by riding a horse" in the Qinghai area. A scholar who took part in the imperial examinations had to first pass local examinations, and only then could he take the national examinations at the capital. Each time he passed one of these examinations, a wearing-hat ceremony was held. Accompanied by the chief director of sacrifices, the official of sacrifices and the master of ceremonies, the scholar would go to worship his ancestors and then paraded in his home village by riding a horse. The scholar and his horse both had red silk draped over them and his relatives and friends followed him. Drums were beaten and music instruments were played. Whenever they arrived a temple, the scholar would enter and burn incense. After this parade, his relatives and friends would hold a banquet and toast the scholar.

Many types of clothing in Chinese society use the name horse (*ma*). For example, *majia* is a vest; *magua* is a coat worn by Manchu men during the Qing Dynasty that later spread across the country; and *mada* are the two bags tied on horse's back. Also among the adornments are a horse-tail hat made of horse tails, popular in Guizhou; riding boots traditionally worn by Mongolians; and horse-hoof sleeves, a kind of sleeve worn by the Manchus when they were in full dress during the Qing Dynasty.

8. Sheep

A favorite game for children in China is called "jump over the goat." One or several persons stand with the upper part of their bodies curved at a ninety degree angle, looking down at the earth or grabbing their ankles. These are called the "goats." Another person or several others jump over the "goat" by putting their palms on the back of "goat and leaping over." Anyone who can't jump over takes the place of the "goat."

A game called "hold the sheep by the mouth" is popular among the Kazaks, Tajik and Mongolian ethnic groups and is generally played on joyous days. Divided into several teams, the horsemen gather on the wide grassland. A sheep is placed several hundred meters away. As soon as the game begins, the horsemen rush toward the sheep in order to catch it. Another form of "holding the sheep by the mouth" is played by letting a young horseman rush out holding a sheep while others chase him, some to capture the sheep, some to protect it. In the end, the horseman who gets the sheep and arrives at the goal is the winner. The game is also played by every team selecting a horseman to chase the sheep. The winner kills and cooks the sheep on the spot and shares the meat with others.

The Pumi people of Yunnan have a funeral custom called "going with a sheep." People there believe they should point out the road for the dead so that the soul can find its way back home. To do this, they use a sheep as a replacement for the dead person. On this occasion, a wizard puts a flour image made with butter on a cross made of wormwood and inserts it into a grain bucket as an offering for the ghosts. Then he gives the name of the dead person to the sheep and scatters wine and glutinous rice cakes on the sheep's ears. The family members of the dead person bow to the sheep asking it to drink the wine. At last, the wizard kills the sheep and takes out its heart and puts this on the offering table while singing a "trail-blazing sutra" and a "Maitreya sutra." It is believed that the dead will go back home and meet their ancestors in this way.

The custom of "offering sacrifices to the sheep ghosts" is held on the twenty-third day of the sixth lunar month each year in Yunnan where some Bai people live. Hosted by an elder herds-man, they offer pig heads, cocks and steamed bread to the sheep ghosts. In order for the sheep ghosts to receive offerings and protect sheep from wild beasts, a sheep's wool rug is hung on a stump beside the sacrificial altar.

The custom of "sending sheep" in the sixth or seventh lunar month was once in vogue in the south Hebei area. The sheep was sent by a grandfather or uncle to the daughter's son or nephew. At first the sheep sent was alive, but gradually this was changed to one made of flour. it is said that the custom was related to the story of Chenxiang's saving his mother by cutting open the mountain (in the story The Magic Lotus Lantern, Chenxiang's mother was placed under Mount Huashan). After Chenxiang saved his mother by cutting open Mount Huashan, he wanted to kill his uncle Yang Erlang for so badly treating his mother. In order to rebuild the relation between his sister and nephew, Yang Erlang sent a pair of live sheep to Chenxiang each year. (Yang has the same pronunciation as the word for sheep.) Hence this became a custom for showing a close relationship to one's nephew.

There is a day for sheep on the fourth day of the first lunar month in Hubei, Hunan, Zhejiang and Hebei provinces. It is said that this day is the birthday of sheep. On this day, people judge the good and bad fortune in keeping sheep during the coming year according to the weather: a fine day indicates prosperity, a cloudy day indicates bad luck. On this occasion, people feed sheep with much care to ensure their multiplication.

During the ancient Western Xia regime, a method of divination by using sheep was called "chant incantation on sheep." The way to do it was to lead a sheep at night to a fortune-teller, who burned incense while chanting incantations to the sheep. The next day, the sheep was killed and the fortune-teller divined according to the look of its internal organs. A clear stomach symbolized good luck, while a bloody heart indicated bad luck. Another way of using a sheep for divination was to put a sheep's thighbone into a fire of burning mugwort and judge according to the cracks produced in the bone by the heat. Still another way was to feed sheep with maize that had been blessed and then kill it when it shook its head. After the sheep was dead, it could be judged according to its internal organs.

The Kazak people of Xinjiang have the custom of "offering guests with a sheep head." The host kills a sheep to prepare a feast for his relatives and friends. At dinner, the host first hands a guest a sheep head with its mouth to the direction of the guests, and the host asks the guest to cut the cheek. The guest then gives a piece of the cheek meat to an elder and a piece of the ear meat to one of the youngest persons present, and takes a piece for himself. Then he holds the sheep head in both hands and passes it over to the host.

The Kirgiz of Xinjiang have the custom of "offering guests with a sheep." In order to entertain guests, the host kills a sheep and cuts the sheep's liver and tail into several pieces, scattering salt solution over the meat. The guests eat in order of age. Some give the sheep's head to an elder, and the elder gives the ear to host's children. Some offer the sheep's tail to an elder to show their respect.

The Kazak, Kirgiz and Tajik ethnic groups in Xinjiang have a dish called "whole sheep." Big slabs of mutton are placed on a plate in the form of a sheep. The sheep head is then offered to the guests.

In Mongolia, a whole sheep is one of the most prized dinners for the Mongolian people. First, milk tea and milky food are given, then cold dishes and wine, and last the whole sheep, while the milky food and cold dishes are cleared away. This is the main course and it is used to serve important guests at festivals and weddings.

The Tajik and Uygur ethnic groups in Xinjiang like to drink mutton soup. The soup made from lamb mutton is considered the best. Mutton with steamed buns in soup, a favorite of the southern Shanxi people, is now popular in all northwest China.

The famous winter dish "instant-boiled mutton" is in vogue in north China. Also named a "mutton hot pot," this food has a long history. The "copper hot pot mutton" appeared 1,400 years ago, and the most famous came from Datong in Shanxi Province. The typical way to make instant-boiled mutton is to select the hind legs of castrated sheep. After freezing, the mutton is cut into pieces, and then put in a pot of boiling water with various flavorings, including onion, ginger, garlic and sesame paste, as well as Chinese cabbage, bean curd, and other vegetables. The mutton boiled in this way is delicious and favorable. It is said that the instant-boiled mutton is related to the ancient Mongolian emperor Kublai Khan. Once he was on a military campaign, tired and hungry. He ordered his entourage to rest and make stewed mutton. At that moment, the scout informed him that the enemy was coming. There was no time to stew the mutton, and so the cook quickly cut the mutton into pieces, threw them in the water, and took them out after stirring them among some scattered flavors. Kublai Khan tasted it and gave the dish high praise. He named it "instant-boiled mutton." Since then, "instant-boiled mutton" has become quite popular. The best sheep for Mongolian "instant-boiled mutton" are those produced by the Xilin Gol League. These sheep eat many kinds of grass and drink sweet spring water, so their flesh is tasty and delicate without a strong smell when cooked. The "instant-boiled mutton" of the Donglai-shun Restaurant is considered the best in Beijing. What the restaurant selects are the hind legs of fat sheep, and every piece of their mutton is less than 1 cm. in size. A plate of mutton at this restaurant has more than 70 pieces.

It is also popular among ethnic groups in Xinjiang to eat kebab. These are mutton cubes roasted on a spit and flavored with *ziran*. Today, kebab can be found all over the country.

In some places in Hubei Province, there is a marital custom called a "basket with sheep and wine." The family who cannot buy a mule or horse carries a sheep's leg and wine in a basket to the bride's home on the wedding day as betrothal gifts.

Somewhere of Qinghai there is a marital custom called "serving a sheep head to the guests." The sheep head is used to entertain the people who escort the bride. The bridegroom's side entertains the guests with Chinese date tea. Then they invite the guests to sit in the threshing ground and offer a sheep head for them to eat.

The Xibo in Xinjiang has a marital custom known as "grabbing the sheep bones." After the wedding, the bride and bridegroom are sent to the bridal chamber by relatives and guests while the bridegroom's parents put a sheep bone at the edge of their *kang* (a heatable brick bed). The bridegroom's mother puts two glasses tied with a red string on a plate, one containing water, the other, wine. She switches these glasses again and again so as to confuse the couple. Then the couple are asked to select one of them. The choice of wine is considered to be lucky, and they must then drink three glasses of wine. Next the sisters and brothers of both sides begin to toy to snatch the sheep bone. If the bridegroom's side gets the bone, it indicates the bridegroom is diligent and capable of supporting his wife; if the bride's side gets the bone, this indicates that the bride is good at running her home and will not be bullied by her husband.

9. Monkey

The ancient Chinese Taoists had a self-cultivation method that involved staying up all night on *gengshen* day. (According to the ancient Chinese calendar, there is a *gengshen* day about every two months.) The Taoists believed that there was an insect inside human body called a three-body insect that made trouble for people. As the trouble-maker, the three-body insect reported people's errors to the gods of heaven and earth when they were asleep on *gengshen* day. In order to prevent its action, the Taoists stayed up all night on every *gengshen* day. Hence the custom. In the Earthly Branches of the calendar, *gengshen* belonged to the monkey's day, so in people's minds, this day was particularly concerned with the monkey. When this idea spread to Japan, the Japanese developed a picture called the "picture of three monkeys." In it were three monkeys, one with its ears covered, one with its mouth covered, and one with its eyes covered. These monkeys are often referred to as "hear no evil, speak no evil, and see no evil."

In Chinese, the word for monkey has almost the same sound as that for a marquis. Because the marquis was the second rank and could refer to any official post, people often drew monkeys as a sign of official actions. Some drew a monkey climbing a maple tree to hand a seal, thus indicating the phrase "to be granted an official title (maple sounds much like grant in Chinese); some drew a monkey on the back of horse, indicating the phrase "to be granted at once" (in Chinese on the back also means at once); and some drew a monkey on another monkey's back to indicate the phrase "to be granted one after another generation" (back sounds like generation in Chinese). Because people thought the monkey to be an auspicious animal, many monkey temples were built.

10. Rooster

An ornament called a "spring chicken" is popularly worn in the northern Shanxi and Shandong areas. It is made of colorful cloth by young women just before the Beginning of Spring (one of the 24 solar terms that begins on Feb. 3, 4, or 5. Chinese people used to think of this as the beginning of spring). The colorful cloth is stuffed with cotton, and it has Chinese prickly ash at one end for the chicken's eyes and several colorful pieces of cloth at the other end for the chicken's tail. The ornament is unique and full of rural flavor. Put on a child's left sleeve, the ornament signifies good luck in the new spring. It is thrown away during a fair held on the 16th day of the first lunar month. Children who haven't gotten their smallpox vaccinations yet have soybeans inside their mouths equal in number to their age. This is called "chicken eats soybeans."

The Tujia ethnic group calls the shuttlecock game (played by kicking a small cloth-wrapped ball with several chicken hairs attached to it) "kicking a chicken." During the Spring Festival, young men and women kick the "chicken" together. One person kicks the "chicken" into the air and others try to get it. The person who gets the "chicken" can chase anyone among the players; the pursued opposite sex is always his or her loved one. So kicking the "chicken" is also a media for romance.

There is a rooster day on the first day of the first lunar month in Hubei, Hunan, Hebei and Zhejiang provinces. On this day, people give chickens much care instead of killing them and judge their fortunes in keeping chickens according to weather: a fine day indicates prosperity, a cloudy day indicates disaster.

There is another kind of ornament made for the Dragon Boat Festival. It is called "the Dragon Boat bag" and is found in Jinghua of Zhejiang Province. On the fifth day of the fifth lunar month each year, people use red cloth to make these small bags in the shape of chicken's heart. They put tea, rice and realgar powder in them. Such ornaments are hung on children's chests to prevent evil. The words for "chicken heart" sound much like "good memory," and so the chicken heart bag also signifies a good memory in the child's studies.

In ancient times, the people of Jinghua and Wuyi in Zhejiang Province had the custom of "killing a rooster" on the seventh day of the seventh lunar month each year. This was the day that the mythological cowherd and weaving-girl were said to meet each other for a brief time in the heavens. People thought that if they killed the rooster, there would be no heralding of the break of the day and so the cowherd and the weaving-girl could be together forever.

There is a custom of killing a chicken in order to terrify ghosts on the first day of the tenth lunar month each year in the Henan area. It is said that at that time the King of Hell sends ghosts into the world and they won't leave until the Sweeping-graves Festival of the following year. People believe that the ghosts are afraid of the blood of a chicken, so they kill it on this day.

A custom called "wearing a cloth chicken" occurs after the twentieth day of the first lunar month in Fufeng, Shaanxi Province. Women make little chickens with colorful cloth and let children wear these on their arms all year in order to keep fit.

A marital custom called the "longevity chicken" was once

popular in the Hebei and Shandong areas. Near to the wedding day, the bridegroom's side would prepare a red rooster, and the bride's side, a fat hen, calling them "the auspicious persons" (the word for chicken is pronounced much like the word auspicious). On the wedding day, the bride's younger brother or another boy while those who was under age carrying the hen, followed the sedan until it arrived at the bridegroom's home before the rooster crowed. At that time the rooster was still asleep while the hen was awake, which meant that the hen overwhelmed the rooster and so indicated that the bride would not be bullied by her husband. The rooster and hen were then tied to a table leg and the rooster would be beaten until it was weak. This would indicate that the husband would be kept under control. These two chickens would not be killed but would be allowed to die naturally, so they were called "longevity chickens."

There is a marital custom named "rooster performs" in the coastal area of Southeast. This is a marriage ceremony performed by a rooster instead of the bridegroom. It takes place when a fisherman bridegroom misses the wedding day because he is still at sea. The bridegroom's side then uses a rooster to take his place in the marriage ceremony. Held by the husband's younger sister or the best man, the rooster's head is pushed down to bow during the marriage ceremony. After it is over, the relatives hang a red cloth on the rooster's neck and send it to the bridal room until the bridegroom returns. Hence the saying goes, "His younger sister performs the marriage ceremony; the rooster accompanies the bride to the bridal room."

Taiwan once had a marital custom called "leading-the-way chicken." Before a wedding day, the bride's side selected a strong and pregnant hen and a young rooster which had just learned to crow. Then on the wedding day, her parents would buy two nine *chi* (three-meter) long red string. One end would be tied with the hen's foot, the other, to the rooster's. Then the two animals would be put into a big basket and taken by a bridesmaid to the bridegroom's home. After entering the bridegroom's home, the chickens would be called "husband and wife chickens" and would be a blessing on the harmony and long-lasting love between the couple. The custom also had another meaning, for the chicken was said to have five virtues (politeness, martial arts, bravery, benevolence, and faith), so that the bride should learn from it; while the nine-*chi* long red strings symbolized long-lasting love (nine and long have much the same sound in the Taiwanese dialect). After the bride entered the bridal chamber, the matchmaker or sisters-in-law released the "husband and wife chickens" and put them under the bed. If the rooster came out first, people cheered and said that "the first child will be a boy." If the hen came out first they said, "the first child will be a girl, and who will bring it a brother." So the husband and wife chickens were used to predict the sex of any offspring.

There is a marital custom of "killing the chicken" in the Zhejiang area. On the wedding day when the bridegroom goes to the bride's home, the bride's side puts a white cloth on the ground. The bridegroom is expected to kill a chicken over this cloth without dripping chicken blood onto it. If he fails to do so, he will have to drink wine, one drop of blood for one bowl. Otherwise, when killing the chicken, the bride will strike him on purpose. But the killing process presents no difficulty for a smart bridegroom.

There is another marital custom in the Yangtze River Delta area. The bridegroom presents a big rooster tied with red silk to the bride's side at the wedding. But the bride's side is not expected to keep the chicken and take it back to the bridegroom's home for their wedding ceremony.

There is a marital custom called "holding a hen" in Shandong Province. On the wedding day, the bride's side asks a little boy to hold a hen and follow behind the bridal sedan. Because the word chicken sounds much like auspicious, holding a hen indicates good luck.

People of Hunan have a marital custom of "sending the leaving-mother chicken." The day before a wedding, the bridegroom's side sends a chicken to the bride's side. This chicken is called a "leaving-mother chicken." The next day, after the bride's sedan arrives at the bride's home, she dresses up and the whole family then sits together while the bride presents the chicken with respect to her mother. This is the "leaving-mother chicken," indicating her departure from her mother.

A custom of "making the chicken naked" is popular in Jiangsu and Zhejiang provinces. On the third day of a baby's birth, the child's family kills a chicken and removes its feathers but the internal organs are kept intact. Then they steam it and present the chicken before the image of the heavenly god so it will bless the baby.

There was a custom called "passing the henhouse" in the Qinghai area. If a baby had wet its bed, his mother would hold him in her arms as she passed the henhouse again and again, mumbling, "Brother rooster, sister hen, your baby eats and discharges in the daytime, my baby eats in the daytime but discharges at night. Tonight I pass your house, please let my baby not discharge at night." It was believed that baby's bed-wetting would be avoided in this way. There is another custom in this area. If a newborn baby was suffering from shock, people thought only another life could revive the baby. So they put a rooster at the door of the delivery room and cut its head off and then painted rooster blood on the baby's mouth, calling his father's name many times. When the baby recovered, he was given the nickname Jihuan (meaning the rooster gave its life for the baby).

Many places had the custom of "drinking rooster-blood wine" for the ceremony of becoming sworn brothers. People killed a rooster and put several drops of the rooster's blood into each bowl and swore their brotherhood while drinking the liquid at one gulp.

The Bai ethnic group at Dali in Yunnan Province has the custom of sending "chicken and rice gifts." This involves presenting a chicken and rice wine as a gift in times of childbirth, weddings or building houses. A single gift is a jug of wine and a big chicken; a double gift includes a jug of wine, a jar of grain seeds and two big chickens.

The Miao people of Guangxi have the custom of "becoming related" in their social communication. When a host entertains his guest with a chicken, if the chicken's heart is left in the pot, the guest will become his brother. The host will then give another banquet to celebrate their union. If the chicken's heart is eaten at this time, the host will kill another chicken to serve to the guests. A person who eats the chicken's heart can never be considered a brother.

The Dong people of Guizhou and Guangxi have the custom of "offering guests a chicken head." It is said that a couple once deeply loved each other. When the wife became ill during childbirth, the husband cooked a chicken for her and gave the good part to his wife, while he kept the chicken's head and feet for himself. When the husband became sick, the wife did the same thing. Their son asked why. They told him that the chicken's head and feet were delicious. When this couple died, their son asked the elders of the village how to mourn for his parents. They told him to offer their favorite food in their memory. The son did this. Since then the offering of a chicken's head and feet is used to show respect for old people and it became a custom for receiving guests.

There was a funeral custom called the "lead-soul chicken" in Shanxi, Heilongjiang, Jilin, Liaoning and Shaanxi. When holding the funeral procession, the son or daughter of the deceased walks in the front of the coffin with a chicken in his or her arms to lead the soil. After the funeral, they let the chicken run away and anyone who catches it can keep it.

People in Hunan had a funeral custom called "jumping-well chicken." Here, the term well indicates the hole, or well, of the tomb. Before the coffin was put into the tomb, the deceased's son would prepare a chicken and a geomancer would stand in the tomb well holding the chicken. He would mumble incentations and bite the cockscomb until it dripped blood on a certain spot in the tomb. Then he would continue to mumble incantations. When all was done, the geomancer would throw the chicken out of the tomb, so this is why the chicken was called "jumping-well chicken."

The custom of "chicken tail dinner" is popular in Gansu Province among the Dongxiang ethnic people. They divide a steamed chicken into thirteen parts in the order of the tail, hip, legs, belly, wings and ribs. Because it is thought to be the best part, the chicken tail is offered to the eldest and other parts are served according to age. People who strive for the chicken's tail or a part they are not permitted to eat because of their age are considered to be corrupt individuals.

The ethnic group in Yunnan has a dish named "chicken with thoroughly cooked rice." When rice is almost completely cooked, a chicken and various flavorings are put into it and braised together. Onion is added until all of the water has boiled off. This dish is often made for festivals, offering ceremonies, weddings and entertaining guests.

The Li ethnic group on Hainan island had the custom of "cutting a chicken" to cure a sickness. A red chicken was cut until it bled. The chicken blood was used to prevent evil.

Cockfighting has been a form of entertainment in China since ancient times. It is popular not only among the Han people, but also among other ethnic groups. But cockfighting in different places is done in different ways. At Kaifeng in Henan Province cockfights are held during a fair on the twenty-second day of the first lunar month. The fair ground occupy half a *mu* of land and is surrounded by a four-*chi* high earthen wall. Before the competition, both sides place their bets while spectators shout and cheer for the battling cocks. Gelo ethnic group at Luocheng in Guangxi Zhuang Autonomous Region hold their cockfighting fair during the Spring Festival. At this fair, score is kept by pouring certain amount of water into two pails. The fighting cocks are arranged in order of their size and weight. When the contest begins, if one rooster moves back and the other doesn't chase it, they are both disqualified for breaking the rules. If one rooster moves back, and the other continues to fight, the rooster who moves back loses and is out of the contest. The winner will fight with another rooster. Every round is recorded by water. The rooster who gets the most water is the champion. After the game, the whole village congratulates the winner's owner at his home, with drums beating and cymbals clashing.

In Chinese tradition, many kinds of divination use chickens. The methods vary for the different ethnic groups and places. The Han people offer steamed chickens as sacrifices, and then study the cracks in the two eye bones. The v-shaped cracks are auspicious and the others inauspicious. The Yi people at Liangshan in Sichuan, and in Guangxi, Yunnan and Guizhou uses chicken thighbones, heads, mouths or leg bones for such predictions. When practicing divination, they hang the left and right thighbones, tied with hemp rope, on a wall and judge according to the direction in which they became positioned. The chicken's head was used to predict the weather and disease. A clear parietal bone indicated a fine day; a dark bone, disaster; many black spots, diseases; red spots, a sign of death and blood. The Li people on Hainan island also has a form of "chicken bone divination." They took two thighbones from a chicken and put these on the fork of a little branch and inserted *qian* (bamboo slips used for divination) through the bone hole to judge its direction.

Eating chickens and eggs is not permitted by some ethnic groups, such as the Tibetan Buddhists in Gansu and Qinghai. The Va ethnic group in Yunnan offers chickens and eggs to ghosts, so people are forbidden to eat or to buy and sell this ghosts' food.

11. Dog

There's a custom recorded in China's ancient books that at certain places dogs are favored to have the first taste of newly harvested sesame seeds in mid-summer or rice in mid-autumn, and this custom is still observed by the Yis and the Hanis (two southern ethnic groups of China) as a commemoration rite. This is because they believe their heroic ancestors, who violated the gods in obtaining good rice seed, were changed into dogs. The Yis have a great deal of respect for dogs. For example, they never will eat dog meat, always have a dog well buried when it dies, and their young men like to coil the end of a dog's tail on their heads as a "hero's bownot."

The Zhuangs in the areas of Jingxi, Longlin and Debao in Guangxi Zhuang Autonomous Region usually celebrate their traditional dog meat eating festival on the fifth or twentieth day of the fifth month of the lunar year, for it is believed that the dog's spirit is capable of producing goodness and removing evil, and it often makes its presence on that day.

People at some places in Hubei, Hunan, Hebei and Zhejiang provinces celebrate the Dog's Day on the second day of the first lunar month of each year.

In the old days, the Buyis had the habit of offering sacrifices first to their ancestors and then to their dogs before the meal of the lunar New Year's Day. An elder in each family would place "new rice" and three pieces of pork in a dog's bowl, and then chant sacrificial words while it was eating so as to thank its ancestor's merit for bringing mankind rice seed. It is said there was no rice in the world a long time ago, and it was the clever dog, taken out by its master in search of rice seeds, that brought the stingy god's rice back by secretly rolling on his rice-drying ground.

In ancient times the Mongols made "shooting a straw dog" a rite by which they prayed for good fortune and the removal of disasters. On a day in the late December each year that they stood a straw dog stuffed with colored silk on flat ground and shot at it with arrows. After such shooting, they often offered mutton and wine to it.

Some areas in Zhejiang Province made it a custom to wrap a newborn baby in old clothes and place it in a dog's house for awhile because locals thought that a baby who had lain in a dog's house would grow up as easily as a dog does. The old clothes were used in the belief that a child so dressed when young would be rich enough to wear silk when it grew up. Furthermore such a child wouldn't be spoiled in his infancy.

Children in the Ningbo area in Zhejiang Province like to wear a "dog-head cap." The custom comes from a story that once a newborn baby of an old couple was saved by a yellow dog and the thankful parents made a cap in the shape the dog's head for the baby in commemoration. By and by this custom spread elsewhere.

Butchers in the Xuzhou area never chop dog meat with a knife. There's a story about the origin of this interesting custom. Liu Bang, the first emperor of the Han Dynasty (reigned from 206-194 B.C.) was fond of eating dog meat, but he never paid the butcher from whom he got the meat. So all butchers tried to avoid him. Filled with fury, Liu Bang confiscated their knives so they had to tear the meat by their hands.

In the Hangzhou area of Zhejiang there's a special food called "Qingming Dog," which is made of polished glutinous rice in the shape of a dog during the Qingming Festival (also known as Pure Brightness—the 5th of the 24 solar terms, traditionally observed as a festival for worshipping at ancestral graves). The food is often hung in the room and then cooked with the flowers of leaf mustard on the day for the "Beginning of Summer." It is used as an antipyretic, especially for children.

People living in the east of Qinghai Province use a dog for divination on the first day of the first lunar month of each year. They will put a variety of crop foods in front of the dog so that it can choose one, and they believe the food it chooses to taste is a sure sign of a bumper harvest for that crop in the coming year.

12. Pig

Many places in China have the custom of killing a pig before the Spring Festival to serve as a dainty food or for a sacrifice. People like to eat pork to celebrate the Spring Festival, so pig butchering can be seen almost everywhere in the countryside from the middle of the last month of the lunar year to the eve of the Spring Festival. Some people in Shandong and Shanxi used to butcher a pig as a reward for the kindness of god. For example, a sick person often made a vow to one of the gods that if the sick person got well under blessings from that god they would butcher a pig at the Spring Festival and burn special yellow paper dipped in the pig's blood before the god as a reward. Pigs so butchered are generally butchered before the 25th day of the last month of the lunar year, and the 26th day is called "Day of Sealing the Knife." The people of Zhejiang believe it is inauspicious to slaughter a pig with more than a single stroke. Women and children are forbidden to watch the butchering. When the butchering is finished, the paper stained with the pig blood is placed in the corner of the room or in the pigsty to demonstrate the presence of its spirit. When a slaughtered pig is placed in scalding water to remove its hair, a pipe is used to blow bubbles in the water, signifying that the next piglet will quickly grow fat, and hair is left on the pig's head and tail, signifying a successful beginning and completion. People often cut open the pig's chest after they burn incense and pig hairs to worship the god. Some of the pork will then be eaten during the Spring Festival, and the rest will be cut into pieces and salted for future use.

Paper-cuts made from black wax paper in the pattern of "a fat pig pushing open a door" are often seen attached to the doors and window panes in Hebei Province and Tianjin City. There will be a treasure bowl on the pig's back, which signifies a coming fortune for the household.

In ancient times the names of the most promising scholars who passed the imperial examinations would be written in red ink on the Wild Goose Pagoda by the fellow scholar with the best handwriting. This was called "zhu (red)-bi (writing brush)-ti (write)-ming (name). Since the word pig is also pronounced zhu, and pig's feet ti, zhu ti (pig's feet) braised in brown sauce was considered the best gift for young scholars about to sit for the civil examinations, to wish him the honor of a zhu-bi-ti-ming.

In the western mountain areas of Guizhou, there is a custom called "leading the pig and ox." On the first afternoon of the first month of the lunar year children tie a big stone, which represents the ox, and a small stone, which represents the pig, and pull them home, crying, "I'm leading a pig and an ox home!" This is an expression of the local people's wish for thriving husbandry in the new year.

The Shes in Zhejiang usually celebrate the Festival of Rushing to Be the First Pig every autumn in commemoration of a certain Lady Ma who is said to have helped the locals a great deal in raising pigs. When the festival time arrives, the sponsor invites a theatrical troupe to perform for seven days and seven nights at Lady Ma's Memorial Temple (built in commemoration of the woman). When the performance ends, the spectators who have raised pigs will rush back home to butcher one of them and tie the pig to a wooden stand. When they hear the first shriek of a pig at the temple, they rush there as fast as possible carrying their pigs so that they can win first place in reaching the gate of the temple. They believe that the family that captures first place will have luck in raising a fat pig during the coming year. When all the pigs have arrived and been placed in order of their arrival, the sponsor selects the biggest and smallest one, and has these, together with the winner, gaily dressed and sent back home. The other pigs will also be carried back by their owners. Next morning the relatives and friends of each family will come for a celebration breakfast in honor of the luck brought by the pig. They each give the host a red envelope with some money in it; and after the meal the host pays them back with an amount of pork equal to the money given by each person.

In ancient times the noble Yis, living in the Liangshan Mountains in Sichuan, had the custom of giving each of their slaves half the head of a pig on festival days as a symbol of their ownership over them.

People living in the remote mountain areas of Chongqing in Sichuan used to drive out evil spirits by killing a "sow ghost." When something unfortunate happened to a family or to their domestic animals, the elder of the family would offer a sacrifice to some god for good luck. On a selected lucky day the family would slaughter a sow and put its head, feet, intestines, liver and lungs in a basket in front of the sacrificial table. Then the elder would burn incense and say a prayer. After the prayer, the pork and guts would be cooked and eaten up by the family, which symbolized that the ghost had been eliminated thoroughly and the evilness driven out.

The Yis sometimes use a pig to drive out evil in their houses. When someone in the family has been sick for a long time or something unfortunate has happened to the family, they will plant eighteen peeled willow twigs in the ground in front of their gate and place beside these a pig, a chicken and a pinch of buckwheat. Then they will have a monk exercise the evil by sweeping down the twigs while chanting incantations.

People in Guangzhou like to eat roast piglets at weddings. A piglet, usually weighing from ten to forty *jin*, is preserved by special spice and soy sauce before it is roasted. Its golden brown skin symbolizes the chastity of the bride. When she returns to her parents home after the wedding, she is expected to take a roasted piglet with her; otherwise she will be thought to be unchaste.

The Blangs in Xishuangbanna, Yunnan Province, have the custom of distributing pork shish kebab at weddings. On the wedding day, the families of the new couple invite their relatives, neighbors and friends to the wedding banquet and give them the pork shich kebab, which are a symbol of the uniting of their "flesh and blood."

People in the Chaoyang area in Guangdong used to hang a piece of fat pork in front of the bridal sedan for the sake of safety. There is a legend about this interesting custom: Once during the Ming Dynasty, Li Ling, a native of Chaoyang, told his neighbors who were carrying the sedan to the bride's home that there would be monkeys coming to attack them because it was the monkeys' food-searching day. He suggested they brought some pork with them. When they saw a monkey they could give a piece of pork to it. Later this practice was followed by many other people and became a folk custom.

Some places in Shaanxi have the wedding custom of sending pig's feet. On the day before the wedding, the bridegroom's family will send two kilograms of pork and two pig's feet to the bride's family. The latter will accept the pork but return the pig's feet. On the day after the wedding, the new couple will go to visit the bride's family with two packs of noodles and two pig's feet. Again the bride's family will accept the noodles but return the pig's feet. The coming and going of the pig's feet indicates that the two families' wish for a close relationship between them forever.

The Vas in Yunnan often use pig's gallbladder to practice divination by judging the direction of the lines on it and the amount of liquid in it. They believe that if the lines run vertically and it contains much liquid, this is a good omen; if the lines run horizontally and it contains little liquid, this is an ill omen.

IV. The Chinese Zodiac and Human Characteristics

It is reasonable to say that people's lives are affected by their characters. But the belief that people's character is affected by the animal that is the symbol of the year in which they were born is unfounded. In fact the "twelve animals of the Chinese zodiac" is a concept only created by men. Earlier we pointed out that "the twelve animals" are just the symbols of the years. But during China's long history, the ancestors formed the superstitious belief that people's character resembles the animal in which they were born, and the character of the animal affects their lives. We should point out that when such a superstitious idea is held, it does affect people's lives to some degree, especially for those people who believe in it. Here is an example. There is a saying that "In ten sheep, nine are incomplete." This means that most of the people born in the year of the sheep do not live a happy life. Yet those people who believe in this superstitious belief will pay attention to people born in the year of the sheep, and try their best to find similarities in their lives. This will make them believe in the zodiac theories more than at any time before, and they will not try to find sociological reasons for their own problems. They will say it is all because they were born in the year of the sheep. Thus the belief has affected them. During the long history of China, there have been many Chinese people who believed that their lives were determined by the year in which they were born and this has reflected in the way they treated friends and their concept of marriage.

However this situation is not that simple. Since the concept has existed for thousands of years that each life is decided by "the twelve animals," it seems that it has a reason for existing. The reason is not because the theory is scientific. It is because it reflects a kind of human ideal with deep cultural traditions. People need to find an object of reference in order to know themselves better and to make themselves better. So they created the far fetched conjecture about "the twelve animals" from their own views of life and other human beings. By and by, this conjecture became a firm conclusion, that is to say different animal symbols lead to different characterizations about human lives. Of course, we can't take such theories as true. Only a few people still choose their friends or spouse based on this belief. But people are still quite interested in the relationship between one's life and "the twelve animals," they are willing to talk about it, think about it, and even find themselves in it. This is only because the zodiac is part of the cultural tradition. It still takes a place in modern China culture, and it has its own meaning of existence, so long as it does not spread superstitious belief. So readers should look at the following with care and a correct attitude.

1. Mouse

The following years are mouse years: 1900, 1912, 1924, 1936, 1948, 1960, 1972, 1984, 1996.

The mouse is one of the animals that are found all over the world. It has good vitality and gives people the impression that it is smart, nimble and filled with enterprising spirits.

People born in the year of the mouse share some of the

characteristics of a mouse. They are optimistic, cheerful, do not fall into low spirits no matter how hard the circumstances, and will fight for their lives. At the same time, they are sensitive like a mouse, and have good intuition and imagination, but they are not good at logically drawing their own conclusions.

Viewed from appearances, people born in the year of the mouse are reticent persons, but actually they are not. They are easily worked up, but they can control their spirits. This character allows them to have lots of friends.

People born in the year of the mouse are usually optimistic, cheerful and easy to get along with. Sometimes you may find a person born in the year of the mouse to be critical, complaining and fault finding. But generally speaking, people born in the year of the mouse are easy to get along with. You can find them in circles of close friends and they are usually very friendly.

People born in the year of the mouse treasure their relationships with friends and relatives. Sometimes you will find that they connect their lives closely to those of others. This is because once they like somebody, they can't bear to leave them.

People born in the year of the mouse have a natural instinct for loving money. A boss born in the year of the mouse will care for his employees. He makes sure his employees participate sufficiently in sports and that they maintain a balanced diet. When his employees are sick, he will go to see them. He takes the troubles of employees as his own. But things change as soon as his employees want to talk about raising their wages. Then he becomes a miser. If you want to get money from the person born in the year of the mouse, you will need to bargain with him very hard.

A woman born in the year of the mouse is usually surprisingly frugal. She buys second-hand goods, splits one meal into several, and cuts down on expenses. Of course, if there is real need for money, she will not be stingy.

Sometimes, people born in the year of the mouse live in groups. They don't care if there is another mouth to feed. They will let friends or relatives live in their homes, but they can always find something for them to do. They even let lazy-bones and beggars move in and they provide work for them to do in their houses.

People born in the year of the mouse are able to keep secrets, but they enjoy finding out the secrets of other people. They may use such information as a weapon and are not satisfied until they have achieved someone's destruction. They seek loopholes without feeling shame. In a word, they lose no chances.

Since such a person tries his best to hide his feelings, when his mood changes he will be confused, and not always know why he is angry or worried. The cause may be just because people born in the year of the mouse are active and diligent. They would be unhappy and angry about other people's laziness and waste.

The character of people born in the year of the mouse has its positive and negative side. They are too particular about trifles, criticize others too much and bargain too much. They usually buy things that they don't really need. They are often cheated by others. They also keep many mementos in their rooms, and keep distressed memories in their hearts. Maybe this is because of their desire to accumulate. Although they are willing to poke their noses into other people's business, they mean good.

People born in the year of the mouse have good memories. They like to ask questions and have keen insights. Such a person knows almost everybody and keeps everything around them in mind. Others take it for granted if a person born in the year of the mouse becomes an excellent writer.

People born in the year of the mouse can succeed in everything because they are as clever as mice. They are able to overcome all kinds of difficulties, and face dangers fearlessly. Because of their cool and quick-witted minds, their keen insight and deep understanding of life, defeats in life sharpen their minds and make them out of ordinary.

There is no need to worry about the security of the person born in the year of the mouse. Before he will make any deal, he will leave a way out for himself. In times when things out of the ordinary happen he can overcome trouble almost immediately. An instinct for protecting himself takes the most important place in his heart. Usually his plans take little risk. So if you want to avoid trouble, follow the advice of a person born in the year of the mouse.

Main stumbling block standing in the way of such persons is their wild ambitions. They want to do too many things at the same time, and so they diffuse their energies. If they are able to develop their strong points and avoid their weak points, they will gain great success. Although people born in the year of the mouse are able to foresee dangers, their fondness for bargaining may cause them to draw wrong judgments, and even fall into traps. If they can overcome their greed and be self-restrained, their lives may become plain sailing. But before they realize that greed will do more harm than good, they may suffer at least one disaster of losing a large sum of money. Yet they will not become penniless because they will extricate themselves from such a difficult position.

Among the "twelve animals," the mouse is the most sentimental. So he is not only attached to his children but also to the elder members of his family. Children born in the year of the mouse are considerate towards their parents, trust their parents and forgive any mistakes of their parents. A mother born in the year of the mouse is a good house-wife and can help her husband's work a great deal. However she will spoil her children and will pay too much attention to her husband.

There is an important factor that affects the character of the people born in the year of the mouse. That is the time of day in which they were born. People born in *zi shi* (from 11 p.m. to 1 a.m. the next day) can be pretty and attractive, but are a little bit arrogant. Those born during *chou shi* (from 1 a.m. to 3 a.m.) are slow to action but serious. Those born in *yin shi* (from 3 a.m. to 5 a.m.) are imperious and bellicose. Those born in *mao shi* (from 5 a.m. to 7 a.m.) are gentle. Those born in the *chen shi* (from 7 a.m. to 9 a.m.) are natural and graceful. Those born in *si shi* (from 9 a.m. to 11 a.m.) do not show their feelings. Those born in *wu shi* (from 11 a.m. to 1 p.m.) are full of energy. Those born in *wei shi* (from 1 p.m. to 3 p.m.) are always sentimental and calculating. Those born in *shen shi* (from 3 p.m. to 5 p.m.) are smart and active. Those born in *you shi* (from 5 p.m. to 7 p.m.) are capable and can overestimate their own strength. Those born in *xu shi* (from 7 p.m. to 9 p.m.) are frank and irritable. Those born in *hai shi* (from 9 p.m. to 11 p.m.) are cheerful and look backward and forward. Generally speaking, people born in the night are more hearty than those born in daylight.

People born in the year of the mouse are easily attracted by people born in the year of the ox, thinking they are strong and can be relied on, and those born in the year of the ox appreciate the spirit of dedication of those born in the year of the mouse. The relationship between those born in the year of the dragon and those born in the year of the mouse is usually harmonious. Persons born in the year of the mouse are also attracted to those sharp-witted persons born in the year of the snake, and tend to form coalitions with them. They like the power exhibited by people born in the year of the monkey and appreciate their way of dealing with matters. They also keep good relationships with those born in the year of the tiger, dog or pig.

There may be conflicts between people born in the year of the horse and a person born in the year of the mouse. It is not wise for people born in the year of the mouse to marry a person born in the year of the rooster. The rich imagination of the latter will only make them angry. It may also bring lots of problems for them to marry a person born in the year of the sheep. The warm-hearted and generous sheep will spend all the money a mouse can accumulate.

2. Ox

The following years are ox years: 1901, 1913, 1925, 1937, 1949, 1961, 1973, 1985, 1997.

People born in the year of the ox are steady, plain and quiet. They arrange things systematically and they are patient and tireless. They are usually ready to take other's advice and act with justice. But it is not easy to change their minds because they are stubborn and sometimes prejudice.

Because people born in the year of the ox are reliable and steady, they are trusted by their superiors or persons in authority.

Where there is responsibility, you will always find them. However, they should be careful not to be carried away by success.

Their dauntless character and logical way of thinking is covered up by their plain appearance. Their intelligence and nimbleness are covered up by their reticence and restrained manner. Although they may be introverted by nature, when an opportunity is presented they can become quite dignified and eloquent speakers. They face danger fearlessly, and betray no fear in face of threats. They have a natural and intense trust in themselves. All of these features help them to put everything into order in times of trouble.

People born in the year of the ox do things in an orderly way. They follow settled rules, respect traditional concepts, and always do things the way other people want them to. So people can foresee what they will do the next. They believe that only those who have a down to earth style of work may never be defeated. People born in other years can achieve success depending on their intelligence or other's help. But people born in the year of the ox depend on their own tenacious will and active spirit of devotion. They never believe in chance, keep their words, and once a word is spoken will not take it back even when pulled by a team of four horses (what is said cannot be unsaid). They take an indifferent attitude towards common biases. They will do their jobs with single-hearted devotion, and never give up when something is half-way done.

They are naive when they think about other people's secrets. They cannot fully understand the feelings of others, and seldom cheat others to win their love. Poetry and serenades seldom appear in their lives, even the gifts they give will be durable and practical. Since people born in the year of the ox are quite traditional, it may take a long time for a man born in the year of the ox to propose marriage to a woman. Such a man may be broad minded and maintain good order, but when he proposes marriage to a pretty girl, he will become clumsy and slow in speech. If you happen to be married to him and trust him completely, he will never disappoint you and will be loyal to you all his life. Although he cannot give you mounds of diamonds, or chests of leather clothing, he will try to make your life as comfortable as he can, and never ask for your help.

If you are lucky enough to marry a woman born in the year of the ox, you will find that she is a serious person. She will iron your clothing like your mother once did, never forgetting to fold the newspaper on your desk, and will make you delicious breakfasts. She will be very neat and always punctual. After your marriage you will never lack clean clothing, you will never wear stockings with holes in them, and you will never have to eat burnt food. Thus she will be an ideal wife.

If a man born in the year of the ox feels unhappy about something, this unhappiness will have developed little by little. His memory is precise and can last for a long time. If you harm him, he will remember every detail. People born in the year of the tiger or rooster will complain when they find themselves in adverse circumstances. And those born in the year of the sheep and rabbit will become somewhat sulky. But those born in the year of the ox are different. They will try to reduce their pain and tension through hard work. If they are frustrated in love, they will work hard and refuse the coming "danger" by remaining single.

People born in the year of the ox do not like to owe other people money. The money they repay will be accurate to the last decimal point. And they will have the same requirement of others. If they owe you something without expressing thanks, they will never forgive themselves. You will not get empty thanks from them; they dislike flowery language and flattering words because they think this harms their honor.

People born in the year of the ox are very patient. But they can be horrible if they lose their tempers. At such times they will lose their senses and attack those who hurt them like angry bulls. The only way to cool the anger of a person such as this is to stand away from him and let him cool down gradually. But there is no need to worry, they will not get into a fight unless they are driven beyond the limits of forbearance.

Their words are the rules of their family. They know how to give an order and how to make others follow their order. They hope other people carry out their orders firmly and adhere to their principles on key matters. Although they do not easily become excited, they love their wives and children and they are willing to do anything for them.

People born in the year of the ox have their feet planted on solid ground, and they are not swayed by their emotions. If you ask for their advice on some problem, you will find their support to be quite reliable. All of them have good physiques, and are seldom sick, they trust themselves and never compromise. They show contempt for other's weaknesses.

People born in the year of the ox are born with the ability to lead. They know how to keep people within the bounds of discipline and they are often quite strict. They think one must fulfill one's duty, and do not put barriers in other's roads. Their shortcomings are their stiffness and awkwardness, their calculating nature and their rather standoffish attitude. They are never sly, and do not know how to show consideration for others. They have the qualities of a good soldier. This makes them unsuitable for public relations work and foreign affairs. However people respect them because they are honest, effective, and have a strong sense of principle. If they can try to develop more of a sense of humor and enthusiasm, they will live happy lives.

People born in the year of the ox do not willing seize chances to gain advantage by trickery. They have a strong sense of morality. They never reach their goals in any improper way. They advocate self-reliance. They do not want people to help them. So if you want to give them help, you will have to implore them in order to do so.

People born in the year of the ox are cautious. They like long-term, stable investments. They are not gamblers, and others taking risks only annoy them.

Among the "twelve animals" the colorful character of the rooster will bring sunshine into an ox's life, and become his best friend. Both of them have the spirit of devotion and so they can get along with each other well. The sentimental mouse and the clever snake also can get along well with the ox. People born in these two years will take care of an ox. People born in the year of the rabbit, dragon, and horse, as well as others born in the year of the ox will also have a good relationship with them, but these relationships may not be close ones. People born in the year of the dog may consider the ox very dull because the ox generally lacks a sense of humor. People born in the year of the sheep and the tiger will complain that the ox has too much authority over them.

3. Tiger

The following years are tiger years: 1902, 1914, 1926, 1938, 1950, 1962, 1974, 1986, 1998.

People born in the year of the tiger have a lively disposition and are forthright and uninhibited in nature. They are broad-minded and quick to action. But there is another aspect to their characters. They are full of suspicion, and sometimes will take hasty action. They never hide their feelings. They are honest, tender, generous and humorous at the same time. They are always kind, love babies and animals, and like anything that arouses their imagination.

People born in the year of the tiger usually concentrate on the work at hand. Once they get into their job, they forget all other things, even breathing. You can say they do everything with all their energy.

The lives of sentimental people born in the year of the tiger are usually unconventional and unrestrained when they are young. For some of them, this situation never changes. Perhaps this is because they are happy-go-lucky people, think there can be no practical benefits and they are fearless. They show contempt for the things with which they disagree. They will jeer and scold at a society tied to traditional concepts. They are always eager to show themselves off, and this is one of their most distinct characteristics.

People born in the year of the tiger will never give up no matter how frustrated they may become, or how severe are the misfortunes they meet. Even if there is only one spark left, they will try to make it fire their lives. Their spirits never die out, their lives never end.

When they are under pressure, they may want to depend on someone else. But they still give people the impression that they are in control.

Some people born in the year of the tiger are gentle, sentimental and full of sympathy. Others can be stubborn, selfish and unreasonable.

A woman born in the year of the tiger will be attractive and active. She will have an easy manner. She is good at expressing herself, has a lively disposition, and follows the latest fashions. She may like to spend several hours making herself up, having her hair dressed, and trying on new clothes. If she is at a party, she will have a good time. She enjoys the company of men and she can make them feel free and easy, make them enjoy her company.

A person born in the year of the tiger is selfish by nature. If his self-motive is brought into question, then money, honor, and power will mean nothing to him. When such a person suffers setbacks, he can become very mean. The desire for revenge may drive him to do anything. He can't bear being ignored or looked down upon. Although he can keep calm on important matters, he will lose his temper in such situations.

It is interesting that the two main features of his character are rashness and hesitation, a pair of contradictions. If he chooses the middle road he may become quite successful.

A person born in the year of the tiger is fond of playing. Since he is full of enthusiasm and sentiment, marrying with him or falling in love with him will bring you lots of experiences. He is fond of wrangling. He shows too much desire for possession when he is jealous.

The early life of a person who is born in the year of the tiger may be smooth. In the early years of his growth, he needs to learn how to control his hot temper, which may ruin his life if he does not. During his youth and prime of life he will be engrossed in turning his dream into reality. He will achieve success at last. If he knows how to relax and do things according to the situation, he will spend his remaining years in happiness.

Generally speaking, people born in the year of tiger are mercurial. They can laugh happily one moment, and cry the next. At one moment he will be optimistic but at the next he will lose his heart totally. He may have every sensitive feeling and colorful experience. There is no need to show sympathy for him, and he does not need sympathy. If he is allowed to lead a life according to his choice, he will find endless happiness.

For a person who is born in the year of the tiger, living with a person born in the year of the pig is a happy choice because those born in the year of the pig are honest, gentle and can help the tiger with his shortcoming of acting rashly. Such persons also bring the tiger a sense of security. People born in the year of the tiger can furthermore get along well with those practical people born in the year of the dog. Those born in the year of the dog are loyal, and they can tie down people born in the year of the tiger and make them rational.

People born in the year of the horse have a practical approach and are attractive. They are good friends of those born in the year of the tiger. Both of them are warm and active. Those born in the year of the horse are sensitive, while those born in the year of the tiger are willful. Usually the horse can foresee danger much sooner than those born in the year of the tiger so they can benefit from their sensitive feelings and alert response.

People born in the year of the tiger find it easy to get along with the people born in the year of the mouse, sheep, rooster or others born in the year of the tiger. But they will have conflicts with people born in the year of the ox. They should never challenge the authority of a person born in the year of the ox. These people are serious, never compromise and won't tolerate the tiger's wild actions in defiance of the law. This may doom the tiger should there be a conflict between them.

It is also unwise for a person born in the year of the tiger to marry someone born in the year of the snake because their only common ground will be their suspicious frames of mind. People born in the year of the snake are gentle, calm and timid, while people born in the year of the tiger are insufferably arrogant. It will be most difficult for them to reach any tacit understanding.

One last warning: people born in the year of the monkey are elusive opponents to them. The clever monkey laughs at the tiger endlessly, and the tiger can do nothing but lose his temper when he is thus teased.

4. Rabbit

The following years are rabbit years: 1903, 1915, 1927, 1939, 1951, 1963, 1975, 1987, 1999.

People born in the year of the rabbit are the luckiest among "the twelve animals." The rabbit is a symbol for mercy, elegance, amiability and worship of beauty. People born in this year are kind, speak gently, peaceful, quiet and loving persons. They like to live easy lives. They are reserved persons, love arts and have a strong sense of justice. Whatever they do, they will start well and end well. This feature can make them learned scholars. They are also well adapted to work in government departments, and to be active on the political stage.

It seems that they will turn a deaf ear to other people's advice.

In fact, they may be unable to recover after other people criticize them. To those they love, they are gentle and kind, while to some other people they may be perfunctory and half-hearted, even cool and merciless. Since they are refined and cultivated and self indulgent at the same time, they enjoy their lives, and think their own desires as the most important. They stubbornly believe that it is easy for people to get along with each other. They are always polite and civil even to their enemies. They are disgusted by quarreling and any hostile act.

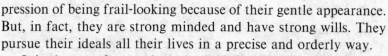

People born in the year of the rabbit give others an impression of being frail-looking because of their gentle appearance. But, in fact, they are strong minded and have strong wills. They pursue their ideals all their lives in a precise and orderly way.

It is also easy for people to get the impression that people born in the year of the rabbit will never do harm to other people. It is true that they seldom use harsh words or say anything rude. They can hide their real features by their decent appearance when they face opponents, and then hurt them. By the time one discovers this, they will have tricked you.

Sometimes people born in the year of the rabbit do things slowly and deliberately. They handle everything in a circumspect way. This is because of their cautious characters. They make certain that they get lots of information before they sign any contract. So they have the ability to evaluate well, and are capable of making clear-headed appraisals of the situation. And they are very proud of this.

A woman born in the year of the rabbit will be serious and considerate. She can forgive the mistakes of her friends. Generally speaking, she will be someone you can get along well. She will be good company with whom to go shopping or to talk. She is smart and warm-hearted. Staying with her will be a happy experience. She will do things she likes energetically, but when she feels tired, she will put aside the work at hand and go quietly away.

A woman born in the year of the rabbit is beautiful and elegant, and she will prefer to be married to a kind, conservative millionaire than to a handsome, penniless man. Her husband must be a person who can provide her favorable material conditions, who can protect her and support her luxurious life style, and who can walk away whenever she is in low spirits.

If she is able to choose her own way of living, she will choose the most comfortable life she can. She will always wear large and comfortable clothing, made of good material. She appreciates harmony and balance, while detesting boasting and dazzling designs.

A man born in the year of the rabbit is solicitous, refined and courteous. He will have a gentle manner and carry himself like a gentleman. People admire his amiability and his resourcefulness, and they will be willing to follow his wise advice. His shortcomings are: unrealistic thinking, high sensitivity, biting, and not being willing to withstand misery.

Since such a person is self-confident, and he will consider himself second to none. In times of urgency, he will discard anything or abandon anyone who dares to disturb his quiet life. He is well known for his flexible and changeable beliefs, and his high skill at maintaining a sense of security.

There is no need to worry about the lives of such people. They are nimble, clever and good at avoiding harm to themselves. They have no lofty ideals to seek. Their main purpose in life is to preserve themselves.

People born in the year of the rabbit are very hospitable, good hosts and warm-hearted companions. Their words make everyone feel happy, but you shouldn't let such words go to your head. They will remember your mistakes, as well as your good points. They know more than they will tell. If your missteps are not serious, they will forgive you. That is why people like them. This philosophy of life keeps them free from troubles, because people will forgive them as they forgive others.

Generally speaking, people born in the year of the rabbit really understand what life means. They make full allowance for other's weal and woe. They know when they should show their forbearance. They never embrace others in public places. They know the art of saving face and giving consideration to the interests of both sides.

People born in the year of the rabbit and sheep are considered the most sympathetic. They know how to comfort others, and will listen to them patiently. They are realists. They will not adventure forth with you into strange places even if you are their best friend. They will help any friend who is in trouble if it is within their power. But if you hurt them they will leave you quickly and in a friendly way.

Their best choice in marriage will be a person born in the year of the sheep. Both of them enjoy material comforts. People also suitable for them are the honest and serious pig, mouse, dragon, monkey, ox and snake. A person born in the year of the rabbit also can marry to another rabbit, but this may be less harmonious. They cannot bear the rooster, who likes criticize others. They also can't bear the bad temper of the tiger, and they can't forgive the changeable horse.

5. Dragon

The following years are dragon years: 1904, 1916, 1928, 1940, 1952, 1964, 1976, 1988 and 2000.

People born in the year of the dragon are full of vitality and strength. To them, life is a colorful leaping flame. Though assuming airs of self-importance, being prejudiced, making arbitrary decisions, and indulging in some of the wildest fantasies, these people are always adored. They are proud, aloof and frank. They establish lofty ideals at an early age, and require others to have same ideals.

In China the dragon symbolizes an emperor and power. It is said that people born in the year of the dragon are powerful. A child born in this year enjoys shouldering heavy loads, even if he is the youngest one in the family, while an older child born in this year often shoulders the responsibility of bringing up his brothers or sisters.

Persons born in the year of the dragon are quite energetic, and their anxiety, yearning, and enthusiasm can be almost as passionate as religious fervor, like the burning fire sprayed by a dragon in legends. They have the potential of achieving great accomplishments, and like to act boldly and resolutely, always putting on a great show as they do so. Although often successful, they are likely to be destroyed and to become self conceited or mad about power if they are unable to control their enthusiasm.

Sometimes such a person will believe that he is greatly restricted by society, tenderness and honeyed words. When he flies into a rage, he can become extraordinarily rude and inconsiderate.

Though his emotion can be as fierce as a volcano, he does not always give himself over to blind emotions. He may act stubbornly and arbitrarily and lose his reason when he flares up. But he will forgive you afterwards and wishes to be forgiven. Sometimes he may forget to apologize. In fact he can become so busy with his work that he will have no time to explain himself. Though hot-tempered and arbitrary, he is respectful to elders. No matter what differences he may have with his family, he will offer his help resolutely and generously, leaving differences behind if his family needs his help.

It is difficult to compete with people born in the year of the dragon, because they are strong and decisive, but not cunning. They like to win success by relying on their own strength, and they are often disgusted with those playing tricks. Due to over-confidence and often misled by illusions, persons of this sort are slow to react to surrounding conspiracies and upcoming dangers, and usually cannot effect countermeasures in time. They are too proud to ask others for help, and will not withdraw even when there is great disparity in strength. They are frank, and never tell a lie.

A person born in the year of the dragon has clear objectives in life, never idling about. He must have a cause to strive for, an objective to be realized, and the opportunity to make mistakes. Without ambitious plans, and the ability to pull his forces together to start afresh after failure, he is like a train that cannot run because of a shortage of fuel.

Women born in the year of the dragon are usually nobel ladies, and will never submit to oppression meekly. They may even outshine men in doing "men's jobs." You can never underestimate such a woman, for she might defeat you or even lead to your destruction.

Judged by her clothes and ornaments, you may find her to be a serious person. She likes practical clothing the most, clothes without ruffles, ribbons, and unnecessary buttons and bows. She loves to wear loose and comfortable clothes, which are suitable for moving about, and dislikes tight ones that are restrictive. In fact, if she is interested in military or public causes, she will gladly wear a uniform.

Such a woman has a strong sense of self-respect. Though she often likes to put on airs, she does not wish others to treat her like a sage. She needs mutual respect among people, and tries her best to respect others.

Though people born in the year of the dragon have many shortcomings, their radiance lights up everyone. They are magnanimous, and never envy others.

Such a person finds pleasure in helping others, and you can always count on their help. They are extroverts who have a deep love for nature, and such a person may become a great travel buff, a good talker, or a sportsman.

The weather at the time a person is born in the year of the dragon affects their later life. If born in stormy weather, such a person will lead a stormy life, which is full of risks, and experience hardships and dangers; if born on a day of gentle breezes and calm waves, such a person will be protected throughout his life and will have a lovely temperament.

A person born in the year of the dragon will either marry early or remain single. He will live a happy single life for he will be preoccupied by his work and career and will often be visited by his worshipers; therefore, he will not feel empty and lonely.

Such a person is neither extravagant nor stingy. In other words, he will be generous and will never care about whether he has made ends meet or not.

Such a person will not keep silent for long, and will struggle to free himself from distress sooner than others will. He is happy, and opposes gentleness. Being firm and persistent, courageous and resolute, he will give the least consideration to the consequences when striving to realize his aim, and will even plunge headlong into an abyss. He sees himself as coming into this world to realize his ideals. The more you might want to make him change his route so as to get around difficulties, the more he will become stubborn. He deserves to be called a pioneer, and will live up to expectations even when in a bad mood.

Such a person is frank, and can never disguise his intentions. He does not guard his thoughts as though they were hidden in a vase to keep secret. Even if he promises not to reveal a word, he may blurt it out when he gets angry.

He has true and sincere love, which comes from the depths of his heart. You can be sure of his true love.

If he is rude, he will probably have a strong destruction force.

People focus their attentions on persons born in the year of the dragon when they are present, and handle affairs according to their thinking. Such a person can arouse everyone's fervor, while he himself does not need to be encouraged, for he is energetic enough. You will never lose faith in an honest "dragon," for he seldom wavers, and will never be terribly suspicious. He has an innate explorative spirit, and tries to succeed at one stroke.

People born in the year of the dragon will have the most tacit understanding with people born in the year of the monkey. A "dragon" and a "mouse" can also form a reliable alliance, for the cunning mouse and strong dragon can achieve a great cause together. A "dragon" can have a happy marriage with a "snake," for the snake with his/her wisdom will prevent the dragon from acting wildly in defiance of the law or public opinion.

People born in the year of the tiger, rooster, horse, sheep, rabbit and pig will try their best to keep company with him for they like his graceful bearing and strength. People born in the year of the dragon can also get along well with others born in the same animal year. However, the relationship between the "dragon" and an "ox" will be tense for they are both quite dignified. The "dog" may give him a headache because he would feel too closely guarded by the "dog," and the "dog" would also be deterred by his power.

Though the "dragon" makes people feel dazzled, he is not a profound thinker, and only when he is able to control the magic power described in legends can he create wonders.

6. Snake

The following years are snake years: 1905, 1917, 1929, 1941, 1953, 1965, 1977 and 1989.

People born in the year of the snake may become philosophers, theologians, politicians, or cunning financiers. The snake is the most enigmatic of the twelve zodiac animals.

Such persons are elegant, and enjoy reading, listening to great music, tasting delicious food, and going to the theatre. They are fascinated with all beautiful things in life. Many of the most beautiful ladies and the men with strongest personalities were born in the  year of the snake. Therefore, you should have good luck if you were born in that year.

A person born in the year of the snake usually acts according to his own judgment, and doesn't follow the views with others. He may be a religious believer or a pleasure-seeker. In either case, he would rather believe in his own conjectures than accept the advice of others, and he is generally right.

They are not annoyed by lack of money, and are usually lucky enough to own everything they need. If such a person is short of money, he can change the situation quickly. However, he shouldn't gamble, for he may lose everything he has. If he sustains great losses, he will soon come to realize his error and recover from it so that he will not be hit later. Generally, he will be cautious and alert when doing business.

These persons are oversuspicious, which is their nature. They hide their suspicions, acting as if nothing is on their minds. They are also generous with money. However, such a person may be famous for heartlessness. To realize an important goal, they may act to eradicate anyone who gets in their way, without any feeling of shame.

Some people born in the year of the snake may speak in a leisurely or listlessly way, but this does not mean that they are slow in thinking and action. They like to think deeply, plan carefully, and make a systematic and appropriate exposition of their views. They usually speak with great care.

A person born in the year of the snake often shows a strong desire for control when associating with others, and can be strict with them. To a certain extent, he will not trust his friends. He will never forgive anyone who breaks a promise. He easily becomes excessively nervous when he is frightened or feels doubtful about something.

When such a person is irritated, he will cherish a bitter hatred. However, he will act with such hostility in a secret way. He shows his resentment with ice-cold hostility instead of bitter words. Some of the people born in the year of the snake may strike their enemies a deadly blow.

A woman born in the year of the snake will be quiet, serene, and have an outstanding appearance. When you look at her carefully, however, you may find that she is not perfectly beautiful. If you look at her facial features separately, you may see that her nose can be too big, or her eyes too close. But she will be quite charming if you look at her in her entirety. She acts confidently and calmly. She often strolls sluggishly, which impresses people by her love of comfort, though, in fact, she is always busy thinking.

Such a woman likes to follow the fashion and be properly dressed. She loves treasures and jewelry. If she has enough money, she will buy the best and real diamonds, pearls, and other jewelry. You would best not give her gold-plating jewelry or replicas, for she may not accept your gift because it seems to be fake.

She is also strict in choosing friends. If she herself does not have power and money, which she advocates, she will often marry a rich and powerful man. As long as her husband has potential, she will try her best to help him to succeed. She acts as a perfect hostess when showing her husband how to make use of every opportunity in his life. With such guidance, support and devotion, the husband will have no choice but to try his best to climb the social ladder.

People born in the year of the snake usually have a sense of humor. In desperate situations, they can enliven the atmosphere with jokes and talk cheerfully and humorously even under great pressure. However, there are some exceptions. Some of these people are icy, some often ridicule others, and some are even grim.

Now you can see that it is not easy to deal with a person born in the year of the snake, especially when he thinks one way and behaves in another. There always lies an alert heart behind his serene appearance. He has a strong will, and will try his best to hold fast to his position. He is so cunning that when you think you may have seized him, he has already slipped away.

Chinese people believe that persons born in the spring or autumn of the year of the snake are the most formidable, while those born in winter are quiet and obedient, for a snake hibernates during winter. Those born in nice weather are happier than those born in terrible weather, and they feel content more easily.

A person born in the year of the snake is a passionate lover, who always makes eyes at persons of the opposite sex. You will make a mistake if you think that such a person is always in love, for they are sensitive toward and yearn for everything, and so their eyes shine with the enthusiasm of first love when they make a good deal.

People born in the year of the snake, especially those who like to be in the limelight and struggle for fame and gain, often lead turbulent lives that are full of passion, forcing them to rack their brains.

The best companions for persons born in the year of the snake are the reliable "ox," fearless "rooster," and heroic "dragon." Such a person can also get along well with people born in the year of the mouse, rabbit, sheep and dog. However, they should avoid the challenging "tiger," and keep only ordinary relationships with the impulsive "horse," who is hard to deal with. The cunning "monkey" will challenge him. Yet people born in the year of the snake can coexist with each other peacefully. However, the sophisticated and tactful "snake" shares no common point with the simple and honest "pig."

As the core force in disturbance and difficult situations, a "snake" will face danger fearlessly, and deal with unforeseen disasters. He has a strong sense of responsibility and clear goals. He may become most powerful if he combines his lofty ideals with inborn advantages.

7. Horse

The following years are horse years: 1906, 1918, 1930, 1942, 1954, 1966, 1978 and 1990.

People born in the year of the horse are sanguine, sharp-minded, dress fashionably, gifted with a silver tongue, and have acute insight. But they fall in the snares of love easily, and break away from them lightly.

Most of the people born in the year of the horse leave their homes when they are young; those who stay at home start their careers early. They are vigorous and energetic. Their most striking point lies in their strong self-confidence, gentleness, and the ability to act as agents in financial transactions.

They do not adhere to old habits and like to show off. In dress, they usually select light colors and peculiar styles, gorgeous but vulgar when they take part in activities or parties.

They like to be engaged in intellectual activities and sports, and people can see this from their skillful actions, graceful posture, and eagerness while speaking. They react quickly and can decide promptly and opportunely. A person born in the year of the horse is generous, likes to join in fun, and are totally easy going persons. They are flexible, active and intelligent, and can usually control others.

However, they are impetuous and stubborn in temperament, and have fiery tempers. Most importantly, they cannot recognize their own weaknesses, and are therefore slow to change. They want others to work as quickly as they do, and if they fail to obtain satisfactory results, they are full of complaints and their faces become clouded. A person born in the year of the horse is always enormously proud of his own success, has many good ideas, and is good at solving knotty problems. He can achieve great success in dealing with chaotic matters. However, he usually feels satisfied and is intoxicated with the small achievements he has made. Moreover, he is often forgetful and absent-minded. Therefore, you should always supervise such a person and urge him on so that he will not become slack.

These people are self-centered and like to be surrounded and served by their relatives and friends. They can channel other people's thinking to their own by using excellent words. And they will not give up until they have poured out all their thoughts, dancing with joy.

People born in the year of the horse believe that their aim in life is to "seek individual freedom and happiness." If you happen to favor this creed, they will not stand at your side for they only believe in their own happiness. However, they are not greedy, selfish, or envious. They will only get angry, but never engage in intrigue or conspiracy when there is trouble on all sides.

Such people are not selfish about material matters. They do not make enemies of others intentionally, but others should not impose their opinions on them. They can scarcely wait when others do not comply with their acute thoughts and agile behavior. They may become excellent actors, but are not suitable to become teachers.

The contradictions in their temperament should be attributed to their changeable moods. They act according to their own intuitions. It is impossible to ask such a person to explain this, or to make a rational analysis of it. However, they can promote the further development of an activity by using their potential, which makes people gasp with admiration. They are often engaged in several activities at the same time, and are good at controlling situations. They put their plans into practice without hesitation once they have made up their minds. They either rush about to devote themselves to their careers, or they become extremely fatigued, and lie down.

It is difficult for a person born in the year of the horse to adapt himself to the schedule worked out by others, and they are too impatient to observe regulations. But they love stimulating jobs.

You should talk to such a person simply and clearly, otherwise he will not concentrate on what you are saying. You should tell him directly whether a plan is feasible or not, and he will appreciate your sincerity and frankness. You should not suppress his emotions excessively, otherwise he will burst into anger, and leave the table or a meeting.

These persons are unwilling to be with people they dislike. They have their own ideas or thoughts, and it is difficult to make them submit to others. They also usually have a large circle of acquaintances and friends, and make new friends every day. But, they never rely on their friends too much.

They are always active in stirring up situations, and can bring about sunshine in winter.

They try to do things quickly, but lack persistence, and they cannot endure hardships over a long period of time. They are flexible, and can adapt themselves to circumstances. When meeting with others, they will not be as blunt as people born in the year of the dragon. For example, they will not visit you without notifying you in advance. On the contrary, they may send you a calling card first, or telephone you before visiting you at your convenience.

A woman born in the year of the horse likes to arrange all things in perfect order. She is so energetic that she would like to appear in ten different places simultaneously, if that was possible.

Her appearance, which may be like a lithe soap bubble, gives people fresh and bright feelings. Some of the women born in the year of the horse are gentle, while others are so arrogant and unyeilding that one can hardly control them. However, they can always win people's appreciation. Family is only a part of their social life, and a woman born in the year of the horse will not always stick to an old place over a long period of time.

She will have deep love for tender plants, natural scenery and pleasant sounds. She has unusual methods for entertaining, and her imagination and passion may be aroused by the roar of the waves and rustling of leaves. She will become overjoyed and full of eagerness when she throws herself into nature. If you fall in love with such a woman, remember not to shut her into your own little worlds.

People born in the year of the horse may be rich, but the property that they own is not safe as they do not worry about protecting it, and therefore they may lose a part of it. They spend extravagantly, and like to make fun of others, both of which are by-products of their imaginative nature. They like to make their marks in the world, and often take the lead when there is nobody else to take responsibility for a decision.

They are quite sensitive to crises of love, and will lose everything if disappointed in live. There are many things that they finish unhappily, and they may experience several broken marriages during their lives.

Those born in summer are usually more able to cope with their lives than those born in winter. When they are middle aged, which are their peak years, they will be capable and experienced, able to bear responsibilities, and scarcely ever fettered.

Their best companions are people born in the year of the tiger, dog and sheep. Those born in the year of dragon, snake, monkey, rabbit, pig and rooster can become their friends, and others born in the year of the horse can get along well with them.

They do not like people born in the year of the mouse because they cannot appreciate their changeable natures. They also have conflicts with people born in the year of the ox, who are stubborn, firm and persistent.

8. Sheep

The following years are sheep years: 1907, 1919, 1931, 1943, 1955, 1967, 1979 and 1991.

It is lucky that the sheep is ranked eighth in the series of Chinese zodiac animals, for the number "eight" in China is an auspicious one, symbolizing peace and prosperity.

Generally speaking, people born in the year of sheep are generous, just and kind, and easily touched by other

people's misfortunes. They are meek, and somewhat timid by nature. When everything goes extremely smoothly in their lives, they appear graceful, if they are artists, and are creative, if they are workers. If something goes especially wrong in their careers or other aspects of life, they will become very sentimental and pessimistic, even world weary.

Behaving gracefully and kind-heartedly, they are always respected and admired by others. They are used to guiding their own conduct by liberal rules as well as treating others with leniency. Besides being good housekeepers, they are also fond of children and pets. Though mild in disposition, they never yield under pressure. It is impossible to force them to do something. When coerced, they will behave in an intransigent way; and when challenged in an argument, they will remain silently anger rather than repeat their opinions or show their displeasure.

Pure and kind as they are, they are always ready to help others who are in need of care or money. Throughout their lives they never worry about the three necessities: food, housing and clothes. Wherever they go, they will make friends with other people, and they will treat their colleagues honestly. Those born in the year of sheep are destined to have good marriages. They will be loved not only by their spouses, but also by family relatives.

It is said people born in the winter of the year of sheep will go on rough and rugged paths throughout life, for winter is a season without the green grass that sheep to live on. Actually, whatever adversity they find themselves in, they needn't be too worried, for other people are always willing to help them. Even when they are in abject poverty they can survive on material donations from their parents or relatives, or through social protection and promotion from the rich and powerful. In all, people born in the year of the sheep can easily get out of difficulties and failures with the help of others who love them.

They like to do things that they are interested in, and realize their dreams in a natural way. When there's something they are unwilling to do, they always refuse with the greatest gentleness and patience. No one knows their true feelings on such occasions, unless they are in rage. As a matter of fact, they are good at settling disputes and creating a harmonious atmosphere around themselves.

They seldom speak in a straightforward way, especially the less well-bred ones among them, which often annoys other people. Never count on them to pour out everything on their minds at once. People must get to know them little by little. In order to encourage them to say more, people should nod from time to time to show their agreement, and always leave some leeway out for them.

It's best for people born in the year of sheep to cooperate with someone who has a strong character. Only under strict working rules and the leadership of hard-minded colleagues, can they make full use of their abilities and work efficiently. So it's best to help them get rid of their "dependent mentality."

They like to live within their usual circle. They attach great importance to their families, favorite foods, birthdays and other festivals. They usually celebrate such special occasions in a showy way, and they are extremely serious about their own birthdays. They may feel heart-broken if they get no congratulations from others.

It seems that people born in the year of sheep are melancholy and sentimental by nature. They always look upon the world passively. Besides, they are used to counting on others to cheer them up. it is easy for them to get lost and to be blue when frustrated, and to make improper choices when going shopping.

Young women born in the year of sheep like to appear sharp. They have a special interest in clothes with ruffles and orna-ments. Every day they spend much time in making themselves up. They always behave in an elegant and orderly way. Besides, they like to decorate their rooms with fresh flowers, which adds to their beauty and vigor. The middle-aged women born in the year of the sheep pay great attention to personal sanitation. They are always neatly and well dressed.

Young women born in the year of sheep like to express their love for their sweethearts in a front way. They trust the men they love, and they want to stay with them every second. To those pursuers in whom they have no interest, they will pay no attention. When someone happens to hit their fancies, they will shake hands with them without any seductive behavior. When they talk, sometimes they will mean "no" by saying "yes," and "yes" by saying "no."

People born in the year of sheep are good at covering up their own weakness with petty shrewdness, and in obtaining what they want by clever tricks and hints. They are also talented in the skill of pestering. Their sincere and composed manner and their pitiful looks always prove effective in persuading other people to do them favors.

They never hurt the feelings of their friends. Sometimes they even give up taking part in social contacts in order to avoid disputes. They are sensitive, and often indulge themselves in sentimental illusions rather than jolly parties. They also like to attract others' attention and flattery regarding their talent. They would be wise to take up professions that enable them to use their strong points. Often doing some down-to-earth job is the best choice for them.

If they're not born during hours dominated by zodiac animals such as dragon, snake or tiger (every two hours of a day is dominated by a different zodiac animal according to the traditional Chinese timing system), they will not be qualified for jobs requiring a strong sense of responsibility and quick decisions. They may do jobs allowing them to have their own way within the bounds of law.

They need strong and loyal companions throughout life. People born in the year of the horse, generally extroverts and emotionalists, and those born in the year of the snake, dragon, monkey and rooster, whose characters are complementary with people born in the year of the sheep, are ideal choices.

Those born in the year of the mouse will be sick of the extravagance and cowardice of people born in the year of the sheep, while those born in the year of the ox, who are reserved and steady by nature, and those born in the year of the dog, who are always vivacious, will have no patience in listening to the chatter of the "sheep," and will seldom understand, sympathize or befriend a "sheep."

9. Monkey

The following years are monkey years: 1908, 1920, 1932, 1944, 1956, 1968, 1980 and 1992.

People born in the year of the monkey can cope with almost any intricacy with a sober mind. Ambitious and knowledgeable as they are, they can achieve great success in whatever career they decide to embrace.

However, they have their weak points, such as a strong sense of superiority, egoism and vanity. So it is easy for them to become jealous when others achieve something or acquire something they don't have.

They also have strong sense of competition and planning, but always keep this a secret. Their talent in seeking wealth, planning for success and demonstrating power cannot be compared with people born in the years of the other zodiac animals.

One of the character traits of people born in the year of the monkey is the firmness. Though some of them appear to be shy, they are adamant inside.

They like to appreciate and show their wit and bravery. They take it for granted that other people are nothing in comparison with them, and they never conceal their happiness and pride. But sometimes their cleverness may overreach itself. When they are playing petty tricks to get something profitable with the least effort and money, or putting forward some shrewd proposals, people may become suspicious of their motives and moral qualities.

Certainly this doesn't mean that they are good for nothing. If we look at them from another angle, we find that their weak points somewhat reflect their intelligence. When they direct their wisdom into the proper channels, they blaze many new trails and initiate various kinds of inventions. Moreover, since they are always in high spirits whether they have failed or not, and are determined to manage their business with great perseverance, they achieve marvelous things in the end.

Monkey people usually adopt the policy of making large sales at a small profit when doing business. Unlike the generous "tigers" and hard-headed "dragons," the "monkeys" square accounts in every detail and accumulate much wealth by saving small profits. Their acumen and economic success are really surprising!

Being ever-victorious, they are never satisfied with what they have had. They want have a try at everything, and never waste a second in doing their work.

They have a strong sense of self-protection. If surrounded, they will try their best to quickly break through any encirclement. Generally speaking they behave carefully and evenly. But when they are incessantly harassed, they will fly into a rage.

Girls born in the year of the monkey are always in high spirit and full of glamour. Wherever they go, they bring happiness to everyone. Witty and agreeable, they are good partners. At exciting evening parties, recreational activities and sumptuous banquets, you can't miss their busy figures!

They are talented in imitating and acting. Always cheerful and energetic, they go straight toward their life aims with indomitable spirits. They never tell their secrets to those who are not their friends, though they speak in a loud voice.

Though fun-lovers, they never waste time in doing something to no avail. They're good at using well-chosen fictions when chatting with different people on different occasions, and taking advantage of other people's weaknesses to control them. As they are perfectionists, it's difficult for their inferiors to please them or take money out of their pockets, unless they have done something perfectly.

Always neatly dressed, women born in the year of the monkey are particular about their appearance, especially their hair styles. By the way, overusing cosmetics may make their skin rough, because it is easy for them to get allergic reactions.

Most of the people born in the year of the monkey have the spirit of working in earnest, and they are good at managing financial affairs. If political or economic circles want to achieve certain aims, it is wise to recruit such people. But only when they're fully on your side, can they be ideal cooperators.

They have some of the characteristics of strategists. For example, they are always ready to seize any favorable chance to achieve their goals, and before they take action they will carefully plan for strategic changes and decent leeways.

They are full of humor and resources, which makes it easy for them to get what they want. But few people dare to believe in and make friends with them because they're generally complicated and mutable and seldom care if they have violated the interests of other people.

To do them justice, they are somewhat indispensable in the real life. Their talent for managing money matters is the admiration of the people born in the year of the mouse, and their wisdom may inspire and enlighten "dragons." Besides, people born in the rabbit, sheep, dog and ox have much respect for their versatility, and the "pigs" and "rooster" like to have them as cooperators.

Of similar character to the "monkeys," people born in the years of the snake and tiger seldom make friends with them, and "tigers" are especially careful not to get involved in the affairs of "monkeys," for this may make them open to attack.

10. Rooster

The following years are rooster years: 1909, 1921, 1933, 1945, 1957, 1969, 1981, 1993.

People born in the year of the rooster usually are good looking and like to show themselves off. Instead of being idle, they always appear to be decent and shrewd in public, even the most timid one of them.

Gossips and more sensible observers (good at watching other people's expressions and weighing their words carefully) are two typical kinds of people born in the year of the rooster, both of whom are difficult to get along with.

But they also have some fine traits. For example, they are shrewd and earnest in fulfilling their duties, talented in doing organizational work, and frank. They are also bold enough to point out and criticize other people's unhealthy activities. Yet inevitably these traits have bad effects, which make these people liable to find fault in others, to show off their intelligence without caring about the others' feelings, and to persist in their own viewpoint in disputes even after such a viewpoint has proven to be wrong.

In addition, they are excellent actors. In a happy mood and nimble manner, they are always radiant and attract others' attentions. They also usually take advantage of any chance to exaggerate their own adventures and achievements. With talent in speaking and writing, they are ever ready to deliver a speech on any topic, and will never give up in argument. So if you want to understand them better, you should tolerate their intrinsic contentiousness. No matter how difficult it may be for you to make concessions, you'd better control yourself, otherwise there will be a hot fight. But to do these people justice, we need to recognize that they are inwardly kind, though they appear to be outwardly contentious.

It is when they are in low spirits that they always wedded to their own ideas, denying any shortcoming they may have. Perhaps they don't intentionally mean to impose their viewpoints on other people, but they put them forward to indicate their own significance. Such obstinate confidence only prevents them from seeing themselves objectively and clearly realizing the harm they may be causing by flaunting and exasperation.

One of their strong points is their capability for managing money matters. They can always make ends meet by careful calculation and strict budgeting. If you're used to spending wastefully, you might ask one of them to keep your money. He will surely help you design a strict financial budget and limit your unnecessary expenditures. With his help, your savings will accrue and your money will be spent in a more reasonable way.

Besides, they excel in housekeeping and tackling troublesome problems. But generally they lack originality, and though good at fulfilling assignments are not pioneers.

Sometimes they will spend extravagantly, but only for themselves. They like to design their offices, residences and themselves in a showy way so as to catch everyone's eyes, and they pay particular attention to their titles and awards, which they regard as manifestations of their greatness. Winning the love of the opposite sex and the favor of their colleagues are other reasons for them to spend money, in addition to decorating their homes.

Generally speaking, they are quite picky, always striving for perfection. They are reasonable, and are good observers of principles, often taking a dim view of those who try to push their way into the front of the line.

When they're too far away from their ideals, they will be quite disappointed. One of their shortcomings is their powerlessness in the midst of setbacks. So they should avoid splitting hairs or going up blind alleys, but should look for other ways to make a better living.

Things are quite different for women born in the year of the rooster. They are most devoted to their duties and seldom boast of their successes. They can do well in any social work, and their colleagues will be easily influenced by their exceptional vitality. Besides, they are patient and kind enough to do jobs that require carefulness and flexibility. They can be good teachers and good wives.

They are used to showing the utmost concern for other people, for perfection in things. They like to give instructions to people who have gone down the wrong path and can't tolerate their losing direction again. If their pride is hurt by others, they will not retort with bitter words; and if they have forgiven somebody, they won't harbor previous ills any longer.

They like to live in a simple and natural way, which is reflected not only in their dress but also in their work.

All people born in the year of the rooster have a good chance to achieve fame because of their competence in the work. They excel in winning their superiors' appreciation by wisdom and high efficiency. But they usually won't try their best to do things they are not interested in.

It's easier for them to gain fame and reward in ordinary posts than it is for others, so they'd better base themselves on ordinary work to fully manifest their capabilities, and they should act with caution in carrying out long-term plans.

They also need to temper their volatile dispositions in a

rigorous and controlled manner so as to remain sober-minded and not involve themselves in disputes. They should listen to other people's opinions modestly to have an objective view of things.

They like flattery and seek the limelight. They are sensitive to criticism of themselves, and always try to defame their opponents instead of acknowledging their own faults.

They show much concern for their families, are gifted with vivid ideas, and have complete confidence in their own ability to achieve success in their work. But they can be dangerous to others because, full of sense of competition, they will drive their opponents into an impasse when they are ablaze with anger.

In a word, people born in the year of the rooster, are usually bloated with pride and are sure to leave a deep impression on others, whether one of respect or one of disgust.

It is interesting that they can get along well with people born in the year of the snake, because their sanguineness and undauntedness and the latter's shrewdness and slipperiness complement each other. People born in the year of the ox also welcome their liveliness because it animates their dull lives, and those born in the year of the dragon like to learn from their far-sighted ambition.

They can also make good friends with the people born in the year of the tiger, sheep, monkey or pig. But there may be fights with others born in the year of the rooster and people born in the year of the mouse. It is difficult for them to have close relations with people born in the year of the rabbit, for their contentiousness will often violate the latter, though they are usually kind-hearted and concessive. Their relationship with people born in the year of the dog is changeable. When their views are identical, they will become close friends, otherwise, they will regard each other as strangers. When necessary, they can cooperate with each other. But if there is a marriage between them, it is doomed to failure.

11. Dog

The following years are dog years: 1910, 1922, 1934, 1946, 1958, 1970, 1982, 1994.

People born in the year of the dog are usually candid, honest, generous, righteous, studious and energetic, which makes it easy for them to attract the favor of the opposite sex.

They are kind-hearted, always ready to listen to and share other people's cares and burdens. They know how to get along well with others. Sometimes they will protect the interests of other people even by sacrificing their own. If there's someone often paying a handsome reward,  he must be a person born in the year of the dog.

They seldom lose their temper, even when they're abused by other people. They do, however, flare up sometimes, but only for a moment, and never out of jealousy. When they have conflicts with others, they always try to make compromises instead of harboring hatred in their hearts.

When they are determined to do something, they will hold on to the very last. They always choose respectful careers, and are sure to achieve success by conscientious hard work.

But never count on them to play a part in settling disputes because they are not willing to involve themselves in such situations. They always guard themselves from abuse, and will only make friends with people in whom they have full confidence.

Being noted cynics, they are highly critical of misbehavior, and are sure to rise up to fight evil in every situation. When they think themselves right, they will not submit to anyone's opinion; and when they have settled something, no one is able to change it. They usually argue in a thoughtful and logical way; but when their integrity's attacked, they will fiercely defend themselves. At the same time, they will never backbite anyone, and they will rush to help when there's danger somewhere.

Gifted with a special sensitivity, they have keen insight into other people's minds. Dividing others into either friends and opponents they will not judge a person without foundation, but once they have developed on opinion of somebody, it is difficult for them to change it. Usually they will give you good advise. Pragmatic by nature, they can help those who boast to overcome their shortcomings. They often think it necessary to point out other people's mistakes so as to help them develop an objective view of themselves and the reality.

Though they don't value money very much, they have an unparalleled ability to bring in money when they are in need of them.

They always appear to be in high spirits, but actually in their hearts there is a shadow of pessimism. Sometimes they worry too much, imagining dangers around every corner.

Women born in the year of the dog are usually strong in thinking. Though plainly dressed, they like nice and fluffy hair styles that make their expressive faces more vivid. They sometimes fidget when angry, but generally they cooperate well with other people and uphold justice. They prefer outdoor sports such as swimming and playing tennis, and they are good friends to their husbands and children, always attentive in listening to their opinions and never getting in their way.

Warm-hearted and easy-going, they are always willing to make friends with other people. These friendships became deepened through usual contacts, such as visits and chats over tea, etc. And they always seem to have the friends in need.

They are energetic and ambitious, and prefer to bury themselves in work that interests them. It's a pity that they lack patience. They seldom get frenzied in love as do people born in the year of the horse or tiger, but they often show the utmost solicitude toward their sweethearts in a quiet way.

It seems that those born in the night are more aggressive than those born in the daytime. But all of them will live a peaceful life with abundance in daily necessities.

They can get along in harmony with those born in the year of the horse, snake, monkey, pig, or even the dog, but not the ox or sheep, and especially not the rooster. They collide with those born in the year of the dragon and never trust them.

12. Pig

The following years are pig years: 1911, 1923, 1935, 1947, 1959, 1971, 1983, 1995.

People born in the year of the pig are steady and resolute in doing things, and honest and warm-hearted to other people. Competent and persistent as they are, they will spare no efforts in fulfilling any job assigned to them.

Though simple-minded, they always have their own opinions. They hope that everything will be peaceful and everyone happy. They can get along well with others because of their leniency and generosity, and they have patience in perfecting themselves and fulfill-ing their jobs, which makes them good teachers. However, they will fly into a rage when forced to, but they never harbor a grudge and stab another person in the back.

They are always faithful to friends and set a high value on

friendship. They have an interest in giving and participating in parties. Besides, they are good peacemakers in others' eyes because of their honesty and trustworthiness.

The more you know them, the deeper your friendship will grow. Besides honesty, they are also warmhearted and careful about their attire. Whenever a friend is in need, they will never hesitate to help.

Their honesty and warm hearts also win them a lot of respect and help, and make them confident and happy.

You may turn to them for consolation and help when you are in low spirits. They will never snub a person, and will help him minimize his troubles.

Women born in the year of the pig like to keep their homes free from dust or untidiness. They have strong characters, paying respect to others as well as to themselves. They may devote all their efforts to succeed in the career they love, oblivious of any reward. Nobly motivated, they keep helping friends afar in secret ways, and host their husbands' friends with great attention and answer children's questions with great patience. People feel at ease with them. The places where you find them are always full of happy laughter.

However, people born in the year of the pig are quite gullible and easily believe in others, even person they know little. So it's a pity that they can't be good treasurers.

They are generous in sharing what they have with others. But they are blunt in speech and actions, sometimes just shrugging off other's insults toward them. And they are near-sighted, only paying attention to the present. No wonder they can always extricate themselves from agony quickly and worry little about misfortunes.

Their kindness to others can't shade their firmness in careers. But success is not easy for them to achieve because they are over-cautious and indecisive.

Honest as these persons are, they usually achieve success by hard work rather than by cheating or stealing.

They have a strong passion and good energy and patience for their work. But sometimes their excessive energy will become the bane of reprobation. When they fail to distinguish the harm in some of the fun they enjoy, they may be easily used by evil people and sink into vice.

They will be hard-working all their lives, sparing no effort in doing everything. Though too much energy will eventually cost them, they can have smooth sailing all the same with the help of their pleasant character.

Their main shortcoming is the fact that they seldom say "no" to others, and always force others to take a mean course in doing things, blurring the line between right and wrong.

They will go into bankruptcy at least once in their lives, but they can manage to retrieve the loss in the end, and they will learn from the experience to become more clever and brave than before.

They often become extremely pessimistic or self-indulgent when they lose everything or lack the ability to help others, the cause of which is their deep belief in fatalism.

Though somewhat cultured, they lack profound insight and usually judge things by appearance alone.

They can live most happily with people born in the year of the rabbit, who are quiet and smart, and those born in the year of the sheep, who are very steady. And they can get along well with those born in the year of the tiger. Besides, they can cooperate with those born in the year of the mouse, ox, dragon, horse, rooster and dog, but not with others born in the year of the pig. They will find themselves at their wits' end when they meet people born in the year of the snake or monkey, because such persons are too wily.

Appendix

Gregorian Calendar	Name of Year by the Heavenly Stems and Earthly Branches	Zodiac Animals
Jan. 31, 1900-Feb. 18, 1901	Geng-Zi	Mouse
Feb. 19, 1901-Feb. 27, 1902	Xin-Chou	Ox
Feb. 28, 1902-Jan. 28, 1903	Ren-Yin	Tiger
Jan. 29, 1903-Feb. 15, 1904	Gui-Mao	Rabbit
Feb. 16, 1904-Feb. 3, 1905	Jia-Chen	Dragon
Feb. 4, 1905-Jan. 24, 1906	Yi-Si	Snake
Jan. 25, 1906-Feb. 12, 1907	Bing-Wu	Horse
Feb. 13, 1907-Feb. 1, 1908	Ding-Wei	Sheep
Feb. 2, 1908-Jan. 21, 1909	Wu-Shen	Monkey
Jan. 22, 1909-Feb. 9, 1910	Ji-You	Rooster
Feb. 10, 1910-Jan. 29, 1911	Geng-Xu	Dog
Jan. 30, 1911-Feb. 17, 1912	Xin-Hai	Pig
Feb. 18, 1912-Feb. 5, 1913	Ren-Zi	Mouse
Feb. 6, 1913-Jan. 25, 1914	Gui-Chou	Ox
Jan. 26, 1914-Feb. 13, 1915	Jia-Yin	Tiger
Feb. 14, 1915-Feb. 2, 1916	Yi-Mao	Rabbit
Feb. 3, 1916-Jan. 22, 1917	Bing-Chen	Dragon
Jan. 23, 1917-Feb. 10, 1918	Ding-Si	Snake
Feb. 11, 1918-Jan. 31, 1919	Wu-Wu	Horse
Feb. 1, 1919-Feb. 19, 1920	Ji-Wei	Sheep
Feb. 20, 1920-Feb. 7, 1921	Geng-Shen	Monkey
Feb. 8, 1921-Jan. 27, 1922	Xin-You	Rooster
Jan. 28, 1922-Feb. 15, 1923	Ren-Xu	Dog
Feb. 16, 1923-Feb. 4, 1924	Gui-Hai	Pig
Feb. 5, 1924-Jan. 23, 1925	Jia-Zi	Mouse
Jan. 24, 1925-Feb. 12, 1926	Yi-Chou	Ox
Feb. 13, 1926-Feb. 1, 1927	Bing-Yin	Tiger

Feb. 2, 1927-Jan. 22, 1928	Ding-Mao	Rabbit
Jan. 23, 1928-Feb. 9, 1929	Wu-Chen	Dragon
Feb. 10, 1929-Jan. 29, 1930	Ji-Si	Snake
Jan. 30, 1930-Feb. 16, 1931	Geng-Wu	Horse
Feb. 17, 1931-Feb. 5, 1932	Xin-Wei	Sheep
Feb. 6, 1932-Jan. 25, 1933	Ren-Shen	Monkey
Jan. 26, 1933-Feb. 13, 1934	Gui-You	Rooster
Feb. 14, 1934-Feb. 3, 1935	Jia-Xu	Dog
Feb. 4, 1935-Jan. 23, 1936	Yi-Hai	Pig
Jan. 24, 1936-Feb. 10, 1937	Bing-Zi	Mouse
Feb. 11, 1937-Jan. 30, 1938	Ding-Chou	Ox
Jan. 31, 1938-Feb. 18, 1939	Wu-Yin	Tiger
Feb. 19, 1939-Feb. 7, 1940	Ji-Mao	Rabbit
Feb. 8, 1940-Jan. 26, 1941	Geng-Chen	Dragon
Jan. 27, 1941-Feb. 14, 1942	Xin-Si	Snake
Feb. 15, 1942-Feb. 4, 1943	Ren-Wu	Horse
Feb. 5, 1943-Jan. 24, 1944	Gui-Wei	Sheep
Jan. 25, 1944-Feb. 12, 1945	Jia-Shen	Monkey
Feb. 13, 1945-Feb. 1, 1946	Yi-You	Rooster
Feb. 2, 1946-Jan. 21, 1947	Bing-Xu	Dog
Jan. 22, 1947-Feb. 9, 1948	Ding-Hai	Pig
Feb. 10, 1948-Jan. 28, 1949	Wu-Zi	Mouse
Jan. 29, 1949-Feb. 16, 1950	Ji-Chou	Ox
Feb. 17, 1950-Feb. 5, 1951	Geng-Yin	Tiger
Feb. 6, 1951-Jan. 26, 1952	Xin-Mao	Rabbit
Jan. 27, 1952-Feb. 13, 1953	Ren-Chen	Dragon
Feb. 14, 1953-Feb. 2, 1954	Gui-Si	Snake
Feb. 3, 1954-Jan. 23, 1955	Jia-Wu	Horse
Jan. 24, 1955-Feb. 11, 1956	Yi-Wei	Sheep
Feb. 12, 1956-Jan. 30, 1957	Bing-Shen	Monkey
Jan. 31, 1957-Feb. 17, 1958	Ding-You	Rooster
Feb. 18, 1958-Feb. 7, 1959	Wu-Xu	Dog
Feb. 8, 1959-Jan. 27, 1960	Ji-Hai	Pig
Jan. 28, 1960-Feb. 14, 1961	Geng-Zi	Mouse
Feb. 15, 1961-Feb. 4, 1962	Xin-Chou	Ox
Feb. 5, 1962-Jan. 24, 1963	Ren-Yin	Tiger
Jan. 25, 1963-Feb. 12, 1964	Gui-Mao	Rabbit

Feb. 13, 1964-Feb. 1, 1965	Jia-Chen	Dragon
Feb. 2, 1965-Jan. 20, 1966	Yi-Si	Snake
Jan. 21, 1966-Feb. 8, 1967	Bing-Wu	Horse
Feb. 9, 1967-Jan. 29, 1968	Ding-Wei	Sheep
Jan. 30, 1968-Feb. 16, 1969	Wu-Shen	Monkey
Feb. 17, 1969-Feb. 5, 1970	Ji-You	Rooster
Feb. 6, 1970-Jan. 26, 1971	Geng-Xu	Dog
Jan. 27, 1971-Feb. 14, 1972	Xin-Hai	Pig
Feb. 15, 1972-Feb. 2, 1973	Ren-Zi	Mouse
Feb. 3, 1973-Jan. 22, 1974	Gui-Chou	Ox
Jan. 23, 1974-Feb. 10, 1975	Jia-Yin	Tiger
Feb. 11, 1975-Jan. 30, 1976	Yi-Mao	Rabbit
Jan. 31, 1976-Feb. 17, 1977	Bing-Chen	Dragon
Feb. 18, 1977-Feb. 6, 1978	Ding-Si	Snake
Feb. 7, 1978-Jan. 27, 1979	Wu-Wu	Horse
Jan. 28, 1979-Feb. 15, 1980	Ji-Wei	Sheep
Feb. 16, 1980-Feb. 4, 1981	Geng-Shen	Monkey
Feb. 5, 1981-Jan. 24, 1982	Xin-You	Rooster
Jan. 25, 1982-Feb. 12, 1983	Ren-Xu	Dog
Feb. 13, 1983-Feb. 1, 1984	Gui-Hai	Pig
Feb. 2, 1984-Feb. 19, 1985	Jia-Zi	Mouse
Feb. 20, 1985-Feb. 8, 1986	Yi-Chou	Ox
Feb. 9, 1986-Jan. 28, 1987	Bing-Yin	Tiger
Jan. 29, 1987-Feb. 16, 1988	Ding-Mao	Rabbit
Feb. 17, 1988-Feb. 5, 1989	Wu-Chen	Dragon
Feb. 6, 1989-Jan. 26, 1990	Ji-Si	Snake
Jan. 27, 1990-Feb. 14, 1991	Geng-Wu	Horse
Feb. 15, 1991-Feb. 3, 1992	Xin-Wei	Sheep
Feb. 4, 1992-Jan. 22, 1993	Ren-Shen	Monkey
Jan. 23, 1993-Feb. 9, 1994	Gui-You	Rooster
Feb. 10, 1994-Jan. 30, 1995	Jia-Xu	Dog
Jan. 31, 1995-Feb. 18, 1996	Yi-Hai	Pig
Feb. 19, 1996-Feb. 6, 1997	Bing-Zi	Mouse
Feb. 7, 1997-Jan. 27, 1998	Ding-Chou	Ox
Jan. 28, 1998-Feb. 15, 1999	Wu-Yin	Tiger
Feb. 16, 1999-Feb. 4, 2000	Ji-Mao	Rabbit

图书在版编目(CIP)数据

中国生肖文化:英文/张方著. —北京:外文出版社,1998
(中国民俗及民间文化丛书)
ISBN 7-119-02064-1

Ⅰ.中… Ⅱ.张… Ⅲ.十二生肖-风俗习惯-中国-英文 Ⅳ.K892.21

中国版本图书馆 CIP 数据核字 (97) 第 10127 号

责任编辑　白雪梅
封面设计　王　志
插图绘制　程星涛

外文出版社网页:

http://www.flp.com.cn

外文出版社电子邮件地址:

info@flp.com.cn

sales@flp.com.cn

中国生肖文化

张方　著

*

©外文出版社
外文出版社出版
(中国北京百万庄大街 24 号)
邮政编码 100037
北京外文印刷厂印刷
中国国际图书贸易总公司发行
(中国北京车公庄西路 35 号)
北京邮政信箱第 399 号　邮政编码 100044
1999 年(大 32 开)第 1 版
1999 年第 1 版第 1 次印刷
(英)
ISBN 7-119-02064-1/G·133(外)
02500
10-E-3216P